C0-AKF-363

24
METALWORKING
PROJECTS

Percy W. Blandford

TAB BOOKS Inc.
Blue Ridge Summit, PA 17214

ATHENS REGIONAL LIBRARY
ATHENS, GEORGIA

421351

FIRST EDITION
FIRST PRINTING

Copyright © 1987 by TAB BOOKS Inc.
Printed in the United States of America

Reproduction or publication of the content in any manner, without express
permission of the publisher, is prohibited. No liability is assumed with respect to
the use of the information herein.

Library of Congress Cataloging in Publication Data

Blandford, Percy W.
24 metalworking projects.

Includes index.
1. Metal-work. I. Title. II. Title: Twenty-four
metalworking projects.
TT205.B55   1986   684'.09   86-14439
ISBN 0-8306-2784-7 (pbk.)

Table of Contents

Introduction

Metalworking takes many forms. Metals can be made into ornamental and decorative objects that may have little practical value, but those are not the projects for some metalworking craftsmen who get the greatest satisfaction out of working metal into practical, functional and mechanical things, which may have a beauty in their fitness for purpose, but which are primarily intended to fulfill a useful role. It is with the aim of suggesting complete projects for the machinist and engineering metalworker that this book has been prepared. Those who favor blacksmithing or ornamental metalwork will find information on those subjects in other books.

In industry, so much engineering metalworking forms only part of some bigger undertaking, and the machinist, toolmaker or other metalworker is denied the satisfaction of saying "I made that," because what he has put into it is only a small part of the whole. In this book, there are 24 complete projects, requiring varying degrees of skill with equipment from basic to advanced. Each is complete, however, and the metalworker should be able to get the satisfaction of making the object unaided throughout.

It is hoped that there is something for all, and the enthusiastic metalworker with access to a lathe and other machine tools should find something that appeals to him and will exercise his skill. There has to be a little woodworking and blacksmithing, but most craftsmen are versatile, and the additional processes should add to interest.

Although the projects are self-contained, this is not an instructional book on techniques. The book is complete in itself, and anyone with ability in machinist's work will need no other instructions. Readers looking for additional instructions are advised to read *The Metalworker's Benchtop Reference Manual* (TAB book No. 2605).

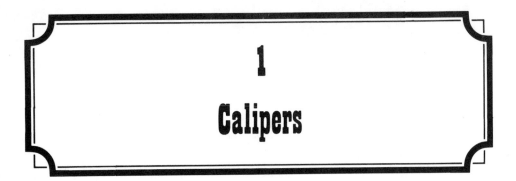

1

Calipers

Calipers of many types are used by other craftsmen and artisans as well as machinists. In some activities, the need for utmost precision is not as great. For most machinist's work, however, calipers should have *micrometer* or *vernier calibrations*. Other workers may get sufficient accuracy by setting with a rule or by test fitting the piece to the part it must fit.

The making of precision calibrated calipers is not usually suitable for one-off and is best left to the manufacturer, but calipers suitable for those with less exact needs make interesting projects. Traditional calipers rely on friction joints to hold the setting. Adjustment is by hand or by tapping the tool on the edge of the bench. The ability of the pivot to allow smooth movement, yet have enough grip to hold the joint at any setting, is the important requirement.

Plain *outside calipers* (FIG. 1-1A) and *inside calipers* (FIG. 1-1B) are used by wood turners and metal turners in making ornamental, rather than precision ground parts. Suitable sizes for this work are 6 to 7 inches from pivot to points. The

arms could be made of 1/8-inch mild steel plate. In both types, the arms are formed as pairs. The legs of the inside calipers may be moved over each other to point inwards for outside use on small diameters.

Mark and cut the outlines, using the pivot points as guides to shape the tops. Give the tips small radius curves so they will bear evenly on work of any diameter. Smooth and round the edges for comfort in use. Drill 1/4-inch holes for the pivot.

Several forms of pivot are possible. The first type uses *integral rivets* (FIG. 1-1C). Turn a washer with a domed surface (FIG. 1-1D). Turn a rivet with a matching domed head (FIG. 1-1E) and a stem long enough to go through and fill the hole in the washer. The countersink in the washer could be at 60°.

Check that all meeting surfaces are flat. Smear with oil. Hammer the rivet end into the countersink and shape its end to match the curve of the washer.

Letting the arms bear against each other

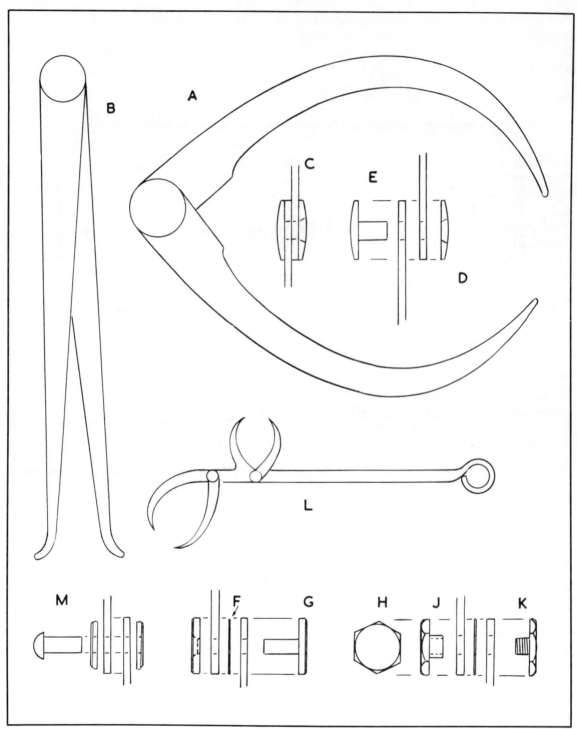

FIG. 1-1. Three forms of calipers and three types of joints.

should be satisfactory, but including a thin soft metal shim may improve smoothness of action (FIG. 1-1F). The rivet parts shown here are chamfered instead of domed (FIG. 1-1G). Use aluminum or copper for the shim. You could use fiber, but that would thicken the joint.

With a rivet, the only way you can tighten a joint (if it loosens after long use) is to hammer it, which may spoil appearance. In practice, the amount of wear is minimal, because movement between the meeting surfaces is slight. The alternative to riveting is screwing, which will permit adjustment or disassembly.

A screw could go through one piece to a tapped hole in the other piece, or it could go into a nut at the other side. In both cases, the arms bear directly on the threaded screw. This may not matter, but it is better to avoid it.

So the screwed parts can be gripped to tighten, give them hexagonal outlines (FIG. 1-1H). Turn one piece with a stem that will not quite go through the parts (FIG. 1-1J). Turn the other part with a stem for screwing (FIG. 1-1K). Provide a threaded hole in the first part to take the second part, being careful to allow tightening before the screwed parts reach their limit.

A blacksmith has to use calipers on hot metal, so he needs an extended handle. Because he might need to check more than one size during one heating, the calipers might be double (FIG. 1-1L).

Make these calipers about 18 inches long, from 1/4-inch plate. The thicker metal is not so likely to overheat and warp or carry heat to the hand. A blacksmith prefers simple rivets (FIG. 1-1M) through washers so he can tighten them on the anvil. The example shown has the handle reduced to a round section and forged to a ring, but that is not essential.

One difficulty with using *jenny* (*odd-leg* or *hermaphrodite*) *calipers* to scribe a line parallel to an edge is keeping the hooked arm level. These calipers have double hooks (FIG. 1-2A), so the upper one bears on the surface and the other on the edge. There is a separate adjustable scribing point (FIG. 1-2B), which eliminates the problem of wear when the point is built in.

The suggested size is 5 inches long and made from 1/16-inch plate. Mark out and cut the legs. Use any of the pivot arrangements already described.

Make the scribing point of 1/16-inch diameter tool steel. Cut a groove for it in the leg (FIG. 1-2C).

Make the peg of 3/16-inch rod (FIG. 1-2D). Drill it for the pin. Use a plain nut, or make a knurled knob to screw on the peg and draw the scribing point into its groove (FIG. 1-2E).

To give friction-joint outside calipers a more exact adjustment and a positive lock when set, there can be left-hand and right-hand threads and a central knurled knob (FIG. 1-2F).

Make the pegs (FIG. 1-2G) of different lengths to allow for the thickness of one leg over the other. On 6-inch calipers, the screwed rod could be 1/8 inch or slightly thicker diameter through pegs 5/16 inch diameter.

Make the knurled knob and braze it to the center of the rod. Cut right-hand and left-hand threads far enough along the rod to allow the intended movement of the calipers. Thread the pegs to match.

The pegs have to turn slightly as the arms open and close. Drill through the arms. Set the pegs along the rod at the correct distance from the knob to suit the setting of the calipers. This is most easily done with the points touching. Put the ends of the pegs through the holes and rivet them over washers (FIG. 1-2H). Alternatively, use nuts on threaded pegs.

Calipers may be made with similar adjustments to that used on some compasses and dividers (FIG. 1-2J). The upper parts of the legs are made 3/8-inch square, then the lower parts taper to round and may be shaped for inside or outside use. A quadrant passes through a slot in one leg and is secured with a knurled screw. Fine adjustment is made with a knurled nut on the end of the quadrant, working against a spring.

Make the legs with extending pieces to overlap at the top (FIG. 1-2K). Cut these circular

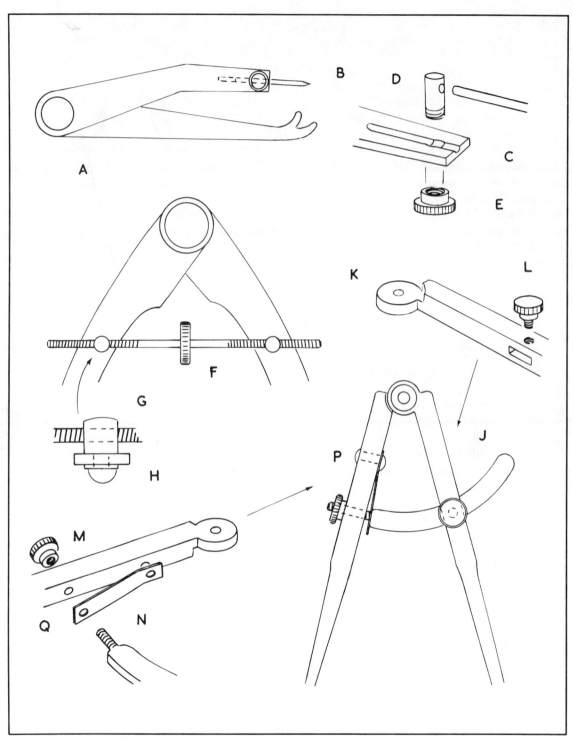

FIG. 1-2. Odd-leg calipers (A-E), screw adjustment (F-H), and arm adjustment (J-N).

to fit into each other. Drill for a rivet to pass through washers. See that this assembly makes a good fit and will pivot correctly before continuing with the other parts.

Make the quadrant 1/8-inch thick and mark where it touches both legs, using the pivot joint as a center for the curve. Cut a slot in one leg to clear the quadrant, and make and fit a screw to hold the quadrant (FIG. 1-2L) at any position.

Drill a hole in a matching position in the other leg (FIG. 1-2M). Reduce the end of the quadrant to 1/8-inch diameter and thread it to fit a knurled nut (FIG. 1-2N).

Make a spring to rivet to the leg (FIG. 1-2P) and bend out about 1/8 inch where it fits over the end of the quadrant (FIG. 1-2Q). Test an assembly of these parts.

Taper and shape the legs. Rivet the top joint and assemble the other parts.

2

Pantograph

A *pantograph* is used to enlarge or reduce drawings, using a system of four bars that can be pivoted together so a tracing point follows the outline being copied and a drawing point repeats the pattern at a different size. The four bars can be pivoted at different points so the ratio between what is being copied and what is being drawn can be varied for a larger or smaller result. Many proportions are possible, but for very great differences of size, the pantograph becomes unwieldly and the risk of error greater. A proportion of 3:1 is reasonable, and this device is intended to enlarge or reduce in a series of steps from not much more than 1:1 up to slightly more than 3:1.

Some pantographs are made of wood, which has the advantage of lightness, but it can warp and pivots might become worn, both affecting accuracy. It is better to use metal throughout. Polished strip brass has an attractive appearance, but for lighter arms aluminum may be used. The arms should be rigid, but of no larger section than is needed to obtain this;

extruded strip 1/8-inch-by-1/2-inch section should be satisfactory. The other parts may be brass, both for the sake of appearance and ease in machining.

When folded, this pantograph is 18 1/2 inches long and about 2 inches wide and thick. It could be made in other sizes, using the same proportions, if you wish.

The arms are drilled and linked with pivots, described as *points* (FIG. 2-1A). Two adjustable points (FIG. 2-1B) link the bars at the chosen intermediate holes. The other points (FIG. 2-1C) differ slightly, but follow similar designs.

For identification, the bars are numbered (FIG. 2-2A). The adjustable points do not touch the paper, but act as movable links. The fixed point has a needle end to push into the drawing board. This is the only point that does not move in use. The main point is just a pivot between arms 1 and 4, but it has a rounded end to rub on the drawing board to keep the pantograph level. The tracing point links arms 2 and 3 and has a metal point to follow the lines of

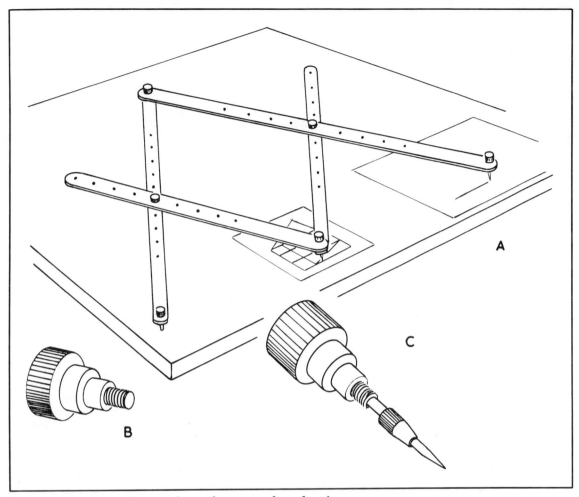

FIG. 2-1. A pantograph is used to enlarge or reduce drawings.

the drawing being copied. The drawing point carries a pencil to make the new drawing. The tracing and drawing points can be changed over, so the pantograph will then make a new drawing to a reduced size.

The four arms have the same hole arrangements, so can be marked together (FIG. 2-2B). They can all be the same length, but there is no need for arms 2 and 3 to be full length, and they may be finished around the last intermediate hole (FIG. 2-2C). Mark the holes, but do not drill until the parts that have to fit them have been made. (Small pilot holes may be drilled through all to ensure uniform spacing.)

Turn the two adjustable points (FIG. 2-1B) from 1/2-inch rod (FIG. 2-2D). The end screws into its hole tapped in the lower arm, the upper arm pivots on the part above it, this is shouldered to hold the bars together, and the top is knurled to provide a grip. Make the threaded end long enough to pass through the lower arm (FIG. 2-2E). Turn the part above it to give just enough clearance on the upper arm, without excessive play (FIG. 2-2F). Sizes of the neck above it are not critical (FIG. 2-2G). Knurl the top and finish it flat or domed.

Drill and tap all the intermediate holes in arms 1 and 3 to suit the threaded ends of the

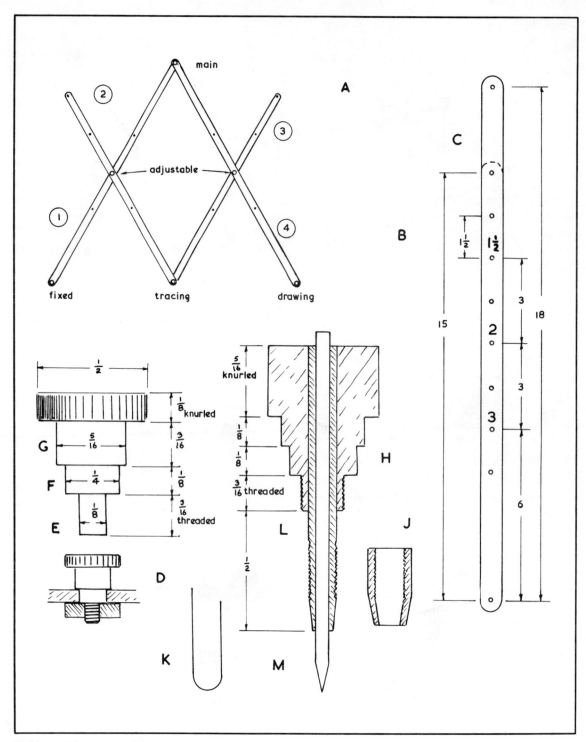

FIG. 2-2. The arm and joints of a pantograph.

adjustable points. Drill and tap the intermediate holes in arms 2 and 4 to fit the shouldered parts above the threaded ends. Check the action.

Punch or engrave the numbers at the hole positions marked on all arms (FIG. 2-2B). These indicate the proportions of enlargement or reduction with the adjustable points at those holes. The other holes give intermediate settings.

It is convenient to arrange the fixed, tracing, and drawing points in a similar way to that used to hold pencil leads in many drafting compasses, with a grip like a small collet chuck. The drawing points hold pencil lead, but the other two grip steel points. The main point could be made in the same way, but it is simpler to make it with a plain end. The tracing and fixed points may be made solid, if you wish.

Each center screws into the lower arm and fits through the one above, in a similar way to the adjustable centers, but through its middle is a tube to carry the steel or pencil point (FIG. 2-2H). Because the diameter of the pencil lead governs other sizes, decide on this first. A convenient size, used in drafting instruments, is 0.075-inch diameter. Obtain tube of this bore or drill rode to suit—three pieces 1 1/4 inch long are required.

At the lower end of each tube, taper the end and make a sleeve to fit over and screw on (FIG. 2-2J). Either taper the sleeve internally or make the hole a reduced size at the end so it grips the tapered tube as it is tightened. Cut across the tapered end and a short distance into the threaded part so tightening the sleeve, using its knurled outside, will compress the tube to grip the lead or rod.

For the main point, prepare a length of rod of the same outside diameter, but about 1/4 inch longer and without a hole. Round its end

smoothly (FIG. 2-2K).

The size of the threaded section of the main parts of the four points (FIG. 2-2L) will depend on how much has to be allowed around the hole, but do not make the diameter any larger than necessary.

Shoulder in two steps above that in a similar way to the adjustable points, but allow a greater depth of knurled top to give a good grip when moving the tracing and drawing points.

Provide threaded holes in both ends of arm 1 and the lower ends of arms 3 and 4. Although the point only goes through one arm thickness at the drawing position of arm 4, the point that fits there is made the same as the others so it can be changed with the tracing point for reduction. Drill clearance holes for the shouldered necks in the arms, which fit on top. Try the action of all parts.

The tubes may be soldered into their upper parts. The extension of the rod at the main point governs the extension of the other points, if it is not made adjustable. Solder it in so there is a gap of about 3/4 inch below the arms.

For the fixed point, make a tool steel rod to pass through its tube. Sharpen it with a needle point to push into the drawing board. For the tracing point, make a similar rod, but with a point at a steeper angle and not sharp enough to scratch the paper. Sharpen a pencil lead to fit into the drawing point (FIG. 2-2M).

For use, set the adjustable points to give the proportions you wish. Push the fixed point into the drawing board. Adjust the other points so the arms ride parallel to the surface of the board. Position the drawing to be copied under the tracing point and plain paper under the drawing point. Make some experimental moves to check that the tracing point will reach all parts of the original drawing and that the drawing point will not run off the paper.

3

Trammels

The name *trammels* is now usually applied to a pair of heads on a beam for use as compass or divider of much larger span than would be possible with normal compasses, but the name really embraces an arrangement of three heads on a beam and a guide which allows the third head to draw an ellipse. A small pair of heads on a metal rod may be called a *beam compass*. For larger work, the heads are mounted on a wooden beam, which may be any reasonable length.

Beam Compass

If the trammels are intended for radii of not more than about 24 inches, the heads can slide on a round steel rod or on a shorter rod that can be extended. For simple dividers, there would be two heads with points. For more precision, there can be fine adjustment on one point. If a pencil is needed, that can be fitted in place of one point.

The rod should be straight steel. The other parts may be steel, but if the heads are polished

brass, except for the steel points, the instrument will have an attractive appearance.

Prepare the rod with a flat at the top (FIG. 31-1A) to take the ends of the screws and prevent the heads from tilting.

For a simple beam divider, make two plain heads (FIG. 3-1B). Drill and tap for a 3/16-inch fixing screw. Taper the bottom and drill and tap for the point. Drill squarely across to slide on the bar.

Make the fixing screws with knurled heads large enough to provide a comfortable grip (FIG. 3-1C). The points are best made of tool steel, with the tips hardened and tempered. Screw to fit in the heads. If a point will not be removed again, it can be turned in tight with a vise, but if you will want to change to pencil or other points, put flats on the sides of the point (FIG. 31-1D) to allow a wrench to be used.

If a fine adjustment is to be added (FIG. 3-1E), lengthen the body of one head (FIG. 3-1F). Make the adjusting head with the same diameter body and fixing screw. Reduce below to 3/8-inch di-

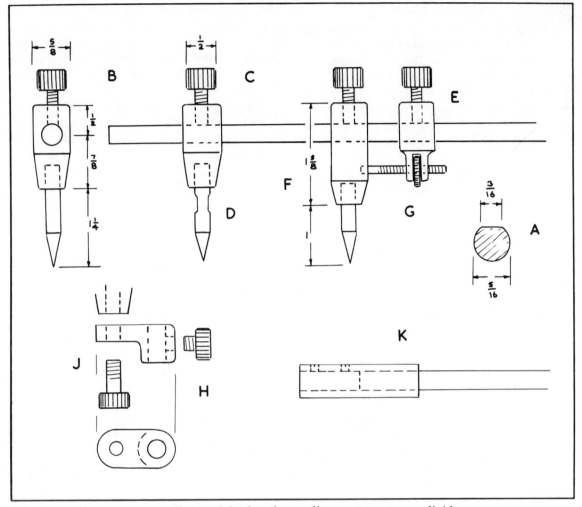

FIG. 3-1. A beam compass will extend further than ordinary compasses or dividers.

ameter, and cut a slot to take a 1/2-inch diameter knurled nut 1/8-inch thick (FIG. 3-1G). Drill across to clear a 1/8-inch screwed rod. Drill and tap the side of the main head to take the end of the rod.

If you wish to be able to substitute a pencil for a point on one head, this can be arranged offset. From 5/8-inch square stock, make a pencil holder (FIG. 3-1H). Drill through a suitable size to take a wood pencil. Alternatively, you could use a holder for a drafting pencil lead (FIG. 2-1C). Reduce the thickness so a knurled screw can pass up through it into a threaded hole in the head (FIG. 3-1J). Round both ends and make the screws.

If most of the use of the beam compass will be at fairly short settings, a long rod can be a nuisance. It may be better to have a rod 10 inches long (or whatever will cover normal use), and then provide an extension for the occasional longer setting. This extension can be a similar rod with a flat top. Make a sleeve to extend over both rods 1 inch (FIG. 3-1K). Drill for screws. These might have knurled heads, but it would be neater to use 1/8-inch grub screws. The sleeve could be attached to the extension piece with more screws, or it may be brazed on.

Trammel Heads

A pair of *trammel heads* to fit on a wood beam may be any size, depending on the distance you hope to span. The size shown (FIG. 3-2) will fit on wood 1/2-inch-by-1 1/4-inch. With straight grained wood, this should be serviceable up to a length of 6 feet or slightly more. On trammels of this size, it is unusual to provide fine adjustment, because they will be used for setting out carpentry, where the need for precision is not as great as in fine metalwork using beam compasses. If a pencil will be needed on one head, that may be provided in the same way as on the beam compass (FIG. 3-1H).

The head is shown with a *pressure pad* under the screw to avoid damaging the wood. The points and screws are 5/16-inch diameter. All of the parts may be steel, or the body may be brass.

The body may be machined from a solid block, but if facilities for cutting the rectangular slot are unavailable, it can be built up (FIG. 3-2B). The parts may be brazed, screwed, or riveted. If they are to brazed, it helps to put pins or thin rivets through near the corners to keep the parts correctly registered while heating. If screwing or riveting, four 3/16-inch diameter should be satisfactory.

Make the pressure pad (FIG. 3-2A) so the recessed part is 3/16-inch thick and the ends stand up enough to keep the pad in place. Drill and tap holes for the point and screw in each head (FIG. 3-2C). Use tool steel for the points and harden and temper the tips. If you expect to want to change to a pencil, put flats for a wrench on one point.

Make the screw with a knurled head large enough to rip easily and of sufficient diameter to project slightly outside the thickness of the head.

Ellipses with Trammels

A complete set of trammels (or *ellipsograph*) consists of a bar with three heads and a crossed

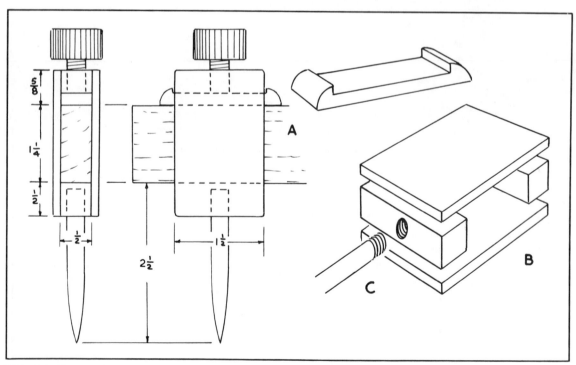

FIG. 3-2. Trammel heads can be made to fit on a wood beam and will form a larger beam compass.

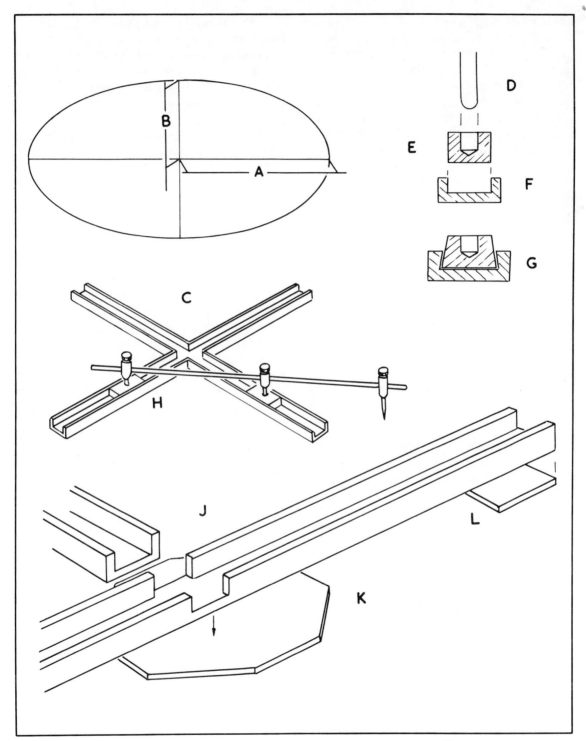

FIG. 3-3. A beam compass or trammels can be used with a guide to draw an ellipse.

guide for two points so the third scratches or draws the ellipse. An ellipse has *major* and *minor axes*. It is the size of the major axis that determines how big you make the parts.

One head on the bar is set to the distance from the marking point equal to half the major axis (FIG. 3-3A). The other is set to half the minor axis (FIG. 3-3B). The size of the largest ellipse you want to draw determines how long the bar is and how long the grooves in the guide must be. A guide (FIG. 3-3C) that is 15 inches overall in each direction can be used with trammels on a bar 20 inches long to draw many sizes and proportions of ellipses. If you make long arms and want to draw small curves, the arms will extend over the circumferences of some ellipses, and short lines will have to be drawn freehand.

Make the three trammel heads and bar as described (FIG. 3-1). On two heads, substitute points with rounded ends (FIG. 3-3D). They need not extend as much as the normal points. The other head may have a point with a tip for scratching or scribing, or it may be fitted with a pencil. The amount of extension of this point or pencil will have to be related to the other points and the guide, when you have made it.

The rounded points fit into sliding blocks (FIG. 3-3E), which fit in channels. The simplest arrangement has the blocks in square-sided channels (FIG. 3-3F), but there would be less risk of unintentional lifting if the blocks and guides were machined at a slight angle—shown here as 10° (FIG. 3-3G).

Because the blocks have to slide across the intersecting channels, make them at least twice as long as the inside width of a channel (FIG. 3-3H). Drill the blocks so the rounded points fit closely but are able to pivot.

Make one channel full-length and the other in two parts. Cut away at the center of the long piece (FIG. 3-3J) so the other pieces fit against it and there is a clear run through. The crossing must be square. You might be able to weld or braze accurately and rigidly without adding any other parts, but there may be a plate below (FIG. 3-3K) and packings at the ends (FIG. 3-3L).

Check the action and adjust the length of the scribing point or pencil so it will mark when the whole assembly is level. Light lubrication might be needed during early use of the apparatus.

4

Three Turning Aids

A turner frequently needs to find the center of a round object, whether he is working in wood, metal, plastic, or any other material. Most of these things are of comparatively small diameter, and the centering head on a combination square (which is often the only suitable device available) might be awkward and clumsy to use. A *center square* no bigger than the palm of your hand is easier to use, with less risk of error.

Center Square

Center squares are based on the fact that if two points on the circumference of a circle are joined, and the resulting chord bisected with a line square to it, that line will pass through the center of the circle. If this is done at two or more positions, the lines drawn will cross at the center.

This center square (FIG. 4-1) has a stock with two arms to bear against the outside of the round object. The points of contact are the ends of a chord, and the edge of the blades bisects

it. Make the stock from 3/8-inch thick steel and the blade from 1/16-inch steel plate. High-carbon steel will make a stronger tool, but mild steel should have a long life.

In the tool, there are three edges requiring accuracy: the two insides of the stock (FIG. 4-1A and B) and the edge of the blade that will be marked along (FIG. 4-1C). The recess into which the blade is set must hold the blade so its edge exactly bisects the angle inside the stock. That angle does not have to be 90°, but it is convenient to make it so.

Cut the stock (FIG. 4-1D) from 3/8-inch steel. A suitable shape for the outside uses 7/8-inch radius at the corner, tapering to 1/2-inch wide at the tips. Make the blade (FIG. 4-1E) a little too long, tapering from 7/8 inch to 1/2 inch.

Mark and machine the recess (FIG. 4-1F) into which the blade can be slid until it is tight. Check that it bisects the stock angle and adjust the edge of the recess, if necessary. Blade and stock surfaces should be level with each other.

Join the blade into the stock with two rivets

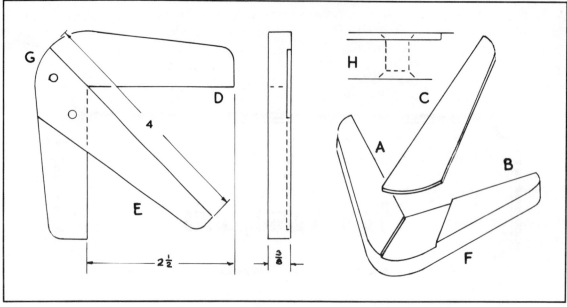

FIG. 4-1. A center square can be used to draw lines square to a circumference or find the center of a circle.

(FIG. 4-1G). Lightly countersink (FIG. 4-1H). If 3/16-inch rod of the same metal as the other parts is used for the rivets, and the countersinks are filled and leveled, the rivet heads should be about invisible.

Bell Center Punch

Although it is theoretically possible to find the center of a round rod down to any size with the center square just described, such things as the width of a pencil or scriber line can affect the result on the ends of small rods. For the ends of small round wood or metal rods it is more satisfactory to use a *bell center punch*. In this, a conical hollow end is put over the rod and a punch point at its apex driven to make a dot.

There are punches that use this principle, in which the punching element is held by a spring. When the point becomes worn, it ceases to be accurate and cannot be removed for sharpening. This bell center punch (FIG. 4-2) is simpler, and the punch can be sharpened or renewed easily. In use, the bell is put over the end of the rod, the body is sighted in line with

it, then the punch is tapped with a hammer. The dent produced can then be deepened, if required, with an ordinary center punch.

The body of the punch (FIG. 4-2A) may be made of tool steel, mild steel, or even brass, if the only use will be on wood or plastic rod, but brass will not last long on steel. The punch should be tool steel, hardened and tempered at the point, but left in the annealed state at the end that will be hit.

The basic punch will mark centers on rods from 1-inch down to 5/16-inch diameter. Bore through a 5/16-inch hole and make the punch (FIG. 4-2B) from rod to slide in it with only enough clearance to allow movement. If the tool is to match the usual lathe center angle, turn the punch point to 60°.

The exact angle of the cone end is not critical. It might be easier to center with an acute cone than an obtuse one, but there are practical limits, and 60° can be used (FIG. 4-2C).

Turn the part to be knurled down to 3/4 inch and reduce each side of that to 5/8 inch (FIG. 4-2D). If the outside of the conical end is made more acute than the inside, that will aid stiff-

16

ness. Round the edges at the mouth of the bell, and polish all but the knurled grip.

If the tool is needed for centering the ends of rods less than 5/16 inch diameter, the punch center can be reduced. It would be unsatisfactory to make the whole punch thinner.

The hole may be reduced to 3/16 inch (FIG. 4-2E) for a sufficient length to guide the punch, which would have to be reduced for enough length to also center larger diameters (FIG. 4-2F).

Make the punch about 1/2 inch longer than the body so there will be enough length to still project when its other end has been shortened by sharpening several times. Bevel the end that will be hit to reduce its tendency to spread under blows.

Depth Gauge

Most *depth gauges* have stocks only long enough for most machinists work, but the turner of wood or spun metal bowls needs to be able to span much wider rims. Great precision is not needed, but a wood turner, in par-

ticular, needs to know the internal depth of a bowl so he can cut far enough without fear of breaking through. The probe can be set with a rule, so the gauge can be simple, providing it is large enough. The suggested gauge (FIG. 4-3) is 12 inches across, but it may be any size.

The stock may be steel or brass, but a machinable aluminum alloy would make a lighter tool more easily managed in use. The probe is tool steel, but it need not be hardened and tempered. The locking assembly would look well in polished brass.

Make the stock from 3/4-inch square material. It would probably work just as well if left square, but shaping (FIG. 4-3A) lightens it and improves appearance. The important considerations are a flat straight bottom and hole for the probe drilled squarely to it. All of the upper edges may be rounded for comfort in handling.

The probe is shown as 3/16-inch rod, 8 inches long (FIG. 4-3B), but other sizes are possible. One end can be rounded and the other pointed. For the broad curve of a wooden bowl,

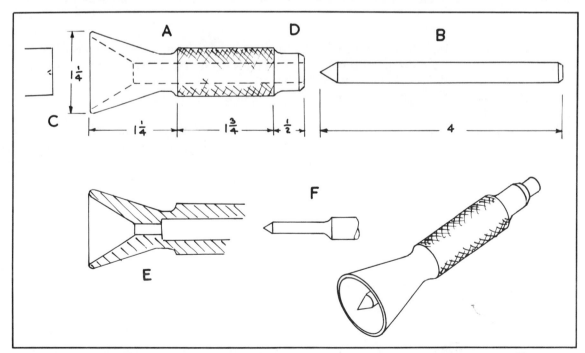

FIG. 4-2. A bell center punch fits over the end of a rod so its center can be punched.

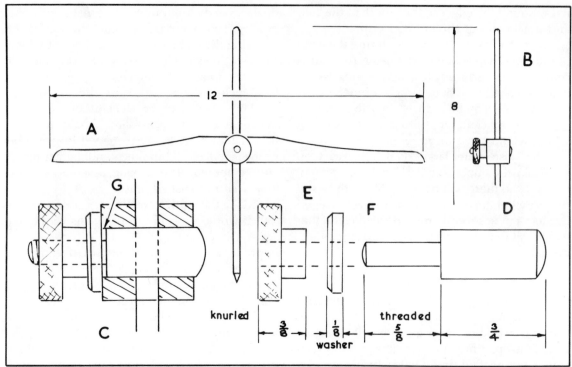

FIG. 4-3. A depth gauge with a long stock is used when turning bowls (A,B). The probe is locked by a screw (C-G).

the rounded end will be the better contact. The point suits narrower and more precise needs.

Drill vertically for the probe (FIG. 4-3C) and horizontally for the 3/8-inch diameter locking bolt (FIG. 4-3D). Make the bolt to slide in the hole and with a threaded end, which could be 3/16-inch or 1/4-inch diameter. Make a knurled

nut (FIG. 4-3E) to fit on the bolt and a washer (FIG. 4-3F) thick enough to take the pressure from the nut.

Position the bolt in its hole so the shoulder is a short distance (not more than 1/16 inch) in from the surface (FIG. 4-3G) and drill through. Fit the probe and try the locking arrangement.

5
Adjustable Bevels

The common *adjustable bevel* used by wood-workers, or the usually smaller version used by metalworkers, has a straight slotted blade pivoting in a stock and a screw to lock the two at any angle relative to each other. It has many uses, but these can be increased if the tool is made with a right-angled blade (FIG. 5-1A). The ordinary bevel is not easy to use at very acute angles. With a right-angled blade, the working edge for an acute angle can be further away from the stock. It also allows any angle to be marked at a distance from the edge. In many marking-out situations, a line at 90° to the first setting is often required. This tool gives it to you automatically. The blade alone can be used as a square for drawing lines at 90° or testing face side and face edge. When one side of the blade is closed into the stock, the other will be square to the stock, and the tool can be used as a try square.

The tool may be made entirely of steel. A brass knurled screw would look good. The whole tool made of brass would be attractive

and noncorrosive, although not as durable as steel. The blade and the top of the stock are made 1/8-inch thick. The bottom of the stock is 3/8-inch thick. It can be lightened with a recess.

Make the blade 6 inches each way, with the ends of each arm cut at 45° (FIG. 5-1B). Cut a slot to fit over a 1/4-inch screw (FIG. 5-1C). Check that the blade arms are parallel and square to each other, inside and out.

Make the two parts of the stock, the same width as a blade arm, to match each other (FIG. 5-1D). At the curved end, be careful that the stock will not project over a blade edge, which might interfere with the use of the tool in some situations. The curved end may be set back up to 1/16 inch, if you prefer it.

The spacer (FIG. 5-1E) should be slightly thicker than the blade to allow easy folding—0.010 extra should be enough. It may be the same width as the stock, but is shown projecting 1/4 inch at one side (FIG. 5-1F). This piece can rest over an edge to take the weight of the stock when marking or testing with the

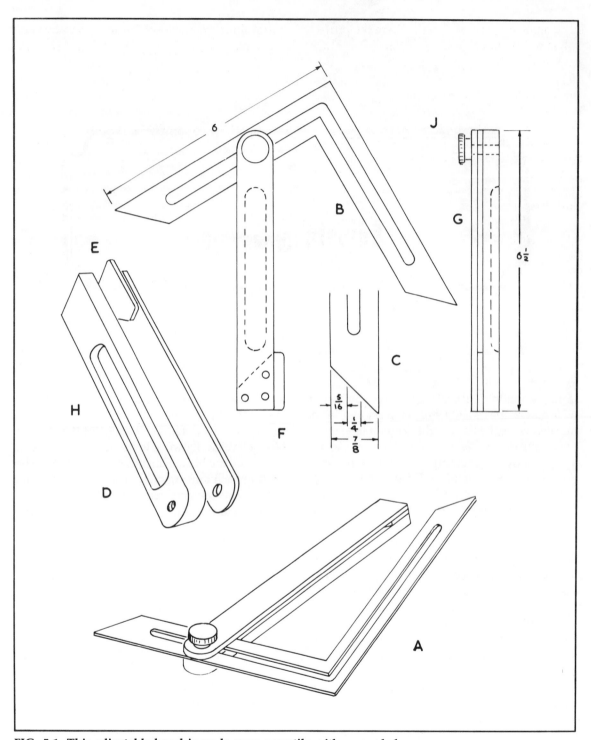

FIG. 5-1. This adjustable bevel is made more versatile with an angled arm.

stock against a side. In places where the projection is not required, the other side of the stock may be used. Arrange the size of the space so one arm of the blade will pivot on the screw and close against it.

If the stock is to be lightened with a recess (FIG. 5-1G and H), machine it with rounded ends to about half thickness. Join the three parts with three rivets, lightly countersunk at each side. If the countersinks are filled with a little metal projecting, the heads can be leveled and will be almost invisible.

Drill through a tapping size hole. Enlarge it to 1/4 inch in the top piece of the stock and cut a thread in the thick part. Make a knurled-head screw (FIG. 5-1J) to suit. Arrange the screwed part so its end is within the thickness of the stock when tight on the blade, so it does not interfere with the flatness of the underside of the stock. Keep the head of the screw fairly thin so there is not much projection on the top of the stock.

Corner Bevel

One situation where the normal adjustable bevel cannot cope very well is measuring an internal angle between surfaces. The woodworker meets this problem when making shelves or furniture to fit closely into the corner of a room. Quite often, the room corner may be assumed to be square, but it is actually several degrees more or less than 90°. That does not matter for normal living, but if something is made 90°, and it extends along unsquare walls, there could be unsightly gaps. Furniture can be made an exact fit if you are able to measure the angle between the walls.

There are other situations with similar needs, as when a bracket has to be fitted between braces or other angular parts. A different sort of adjustable bevel is needed to test these internal angles. A *corner bevel* (FIG. 5-2) can be used inside faces at angles from 110° down to 30°, which will take care of room corners and many other situations. The arms will extend 14 inches from the corner along each surface. The

central slotted part allows the arms to be locked in any position, and it is extended to serve as a handle. That piece also bisects the angle of the arm, whatever their setting, and this fact may be useful to provide a centerline for setting out the shape of a corner shelf or table top.

The tool may be made to other sizes, but shorter arms might not span inequalities in a wall surface, and a very large tool would be heavy and unwieldly. The dotted lines show the positions of the centerlines of the arms and struts at 110° (FIG. 5-2A, B), 90° (FIG. 5-2C, D), or 30° (FIG. 5-2E, F).

Choose strip metal that will be stiff enough without being excessively heavy. The parts drawn are assumed to be steel: 1/8-inch or 3/16-inch-by-1-inch for the central handle; 3/32-inch or 1/8-inch-by-3/4-inch for the arms; and 1/16-inch-by-1/2-inch for the struts. All of the nuts, screws, and washers may be made from 1/2-inch steel or brass round rod.

Make the slotted handle (FIG. 5-3A) tapered to a curve to match the ends of the arms (FIG. 5-3B). The slot is wide enough to slide on a 1/4-inch screw. The end may be left as a rounded piece of metal, but it is shown thickened with wood to make a handle (FIG. 5-3C). The two pieces may be turned as a solid rod, then cut down the middle. Drill for wood screws or take rivets right through the wood.

The two arms are the same (FIG. 5-3D). Shaping of the ends improves appearance, but is not essential. The two struts (FIG. 5-3E) are simple strips with holes at the ends. Their length affects the amount the tool will open and close. If you do not expect to need such wide angles, they could be shortened. The holes for pivots in all strips may be 1/4-inch diameter.

All four pivot assemblies are different. The knurled parts may all be 1/2-inch diameter and 1/4-inch thick.

At the meeting of the struts on the slotted strip (FIG. 5-2G), there is a screw with a washer and knurled nut (FIG. 5-3F). Make the screwed part 1/4-inch diameter and long enough to go through the parts and the nut (FIG. 5-3G). Thread the nut to match. Make sure there is enough thread on the screw for the parts to be locked together.

It is not essential for the other parts to have knurled nuts. They can be tightened with a wrench and may never need to be opened again, but if the nuts can be turned by hand it will be possible to adjust or disassemble at any time.

At the corner joint (FIG. 5-2H), the pivot must allow the parts to move without the nut loosening (FIG. 5-3H). Shoulder the screw (FIG. 5-3J) to a sufficient depth for the three parts to turn smoothly, then the nut tightens the washer on it.

At the strut joints to the arms (FIG. 5-2J, K), the parts come at different levels due to their overlaps at the other joints. Spacers are needed to bring the arms up to levels where they will be parallel and swing evenly for all angles. De-

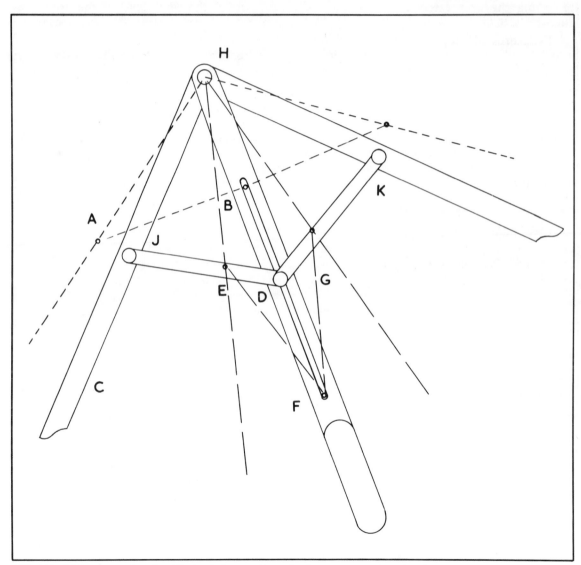

FIG. 5-2. This corner bevel will check internal angles between 110° and 30°.

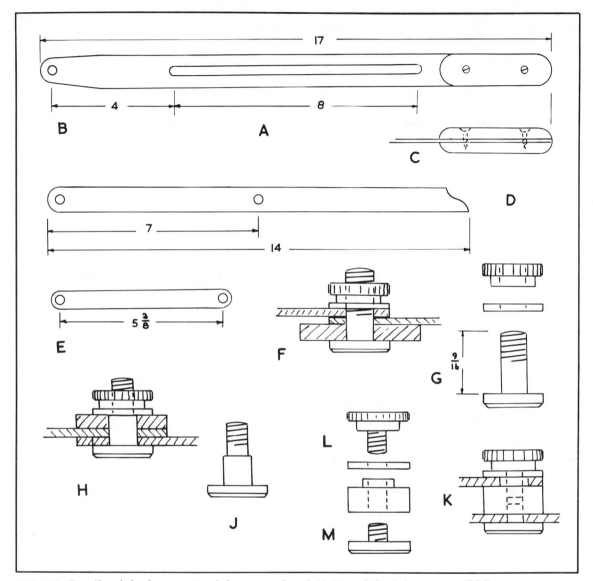

FIG. 5-3. Details of the long parts of the corner bevel (A-E) and the joint screws (F-M).

cide on how the parts will overlap and allow for the combined thickness when making the spacers (FIG. 5-3K). Each spacer is shouldered at the top to fit the hole in its strut, with enough clearance for the arm to move, while the nut holds the washer tight. Drill and tap through the spacers to take screws 3/16-inch diameter, or any other convenient size to pass through the 1/4-inch diameter shoulders (FIG. 5-3L, M).

6

Bar Clamp

Woodworkers and others need to be able to clamp work that is often well outside the range of any C clamps. The type of clamp heads that attach to pipes have their uses, but over longer distances and with considerable pressure applied, the tube may bend and accuracy is lost. It is better to use a bar on edge, which has ample stiffness to resist bending, so the heads are kept parallel even if they are several feet apart. Such a bar clamp has to be fairly heavy and substantial. For many assemblies a pair of clamps are needed. The bar clamp described here will span about 36 inches, so is suitable for most furniture, window frames, and other wooden assemblies in the home (FIG. 6-1).

At the end of the bar is a fixed block, threaded to take a screw (FIG. 6-2A). The end of the screw is attached to a sliding head (FIG. 6-2B). The screw has a lever similar to that of a vise (FIG. 6-2C), and with the amount of screw thread shown the sliding head can be moved 4 inches.

Thrust is taken by a movable head (FIG. 6-2D), which can be positioned anywhere along the bar and stopped by a peg through one of the holes. With possible positions at 2-inch intervals and a 4-inch movement of the screw, there is ample tolerance in adjustment.

The bar in the basic bar clamp is squared-edged steel stock 3/8-inch-by-1 1/2-inches (FIG. 6-2E). This makes a clamp suitable for most woodworking. It could be lighter, and the other parts scaled down, if only small wood working needs are anticipated. The bar could be made longer, without increasing its section, but it then becomes unwieldly when you use it at smaller settings. It may be better to provide an extension bar.

The heads can be machined from steel 7/8-inch-by-1 1/2-inch section, or they may be cast. The two clamping heads are basically similar and made in the same way (FIG. 6-2F). Make the slots a sliding fit on the bar (FIG. 6-2G, H). The pressure pads are 1/4-inch thick and let into the heads 1/8 inch. Cut away to allow for this (FIG. 6-2J).

Mark the position of the hole in the sliding

24

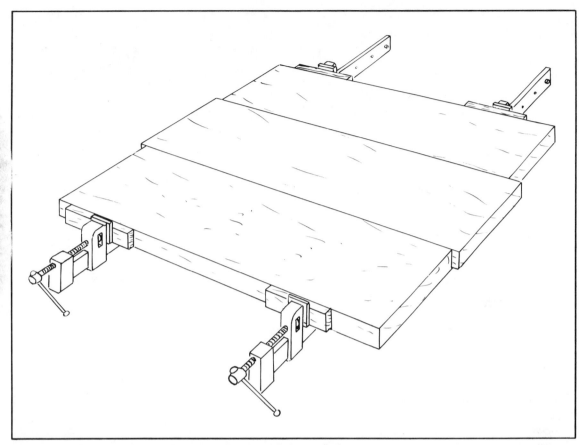

FIG. 6-1. Bar clamps are used where a long reach is needed.

head, and cut the slot to take the collar on the screw symmetrically to this (FIG. 6-2K). On both heads round the edge away from the pressure pad.

Machine the pressure pads all round (FIG. 6-2L). They may be welded on or attached with countersunk screws. Two 1/4-inch screws with their heads just below the surface should hold a pad.

For one or two bar clamps, making patterns and castings for the heads may not be justified, but if castings are used there can be more curves and feet may be included (FIG. 6-2M).

The *screw block* (FIG. 6-2A) is made from the same size stock as the heads (FIG. 6-3A). Machine a slot for the bar in the same way, but because the block does not have to slide, it can be a

closer fit. Mark the screw hole. Round the upper corners. If a casting is used, make similar feet to those on the heads (FIG. 6-3B). The block can be drilled for two rivets through the bar, arranged diagonally (FIG. 6-3C), but if the assembly may never be used reversed for pushing outwards, use a central screw (FIG. 6-3D) so the block can be taken off and located over one of the pin holes when it is turned around.

The screw is made from 1-inch rod, turned down to 5/8 inch for screwing (FIG. 6-3E). Reduce the end to 7/16 inch to fit in a collar (FIG. 6-3F), which goes in the slot in the sliding head and is secured with a 1/8-inch pin. Drill the sliding head to suit and make the collar an easy fit in the opening. The collar and screw end will provide thrust when tightening on work, then pull

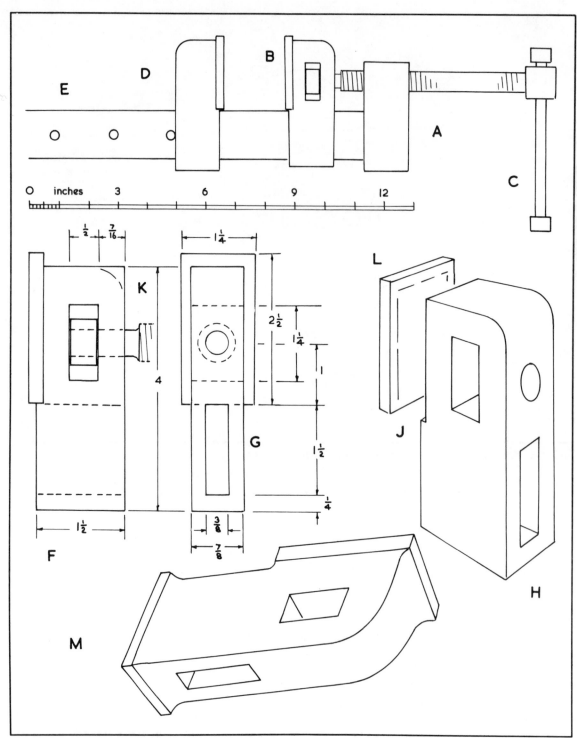

FIG. 6-2. Details of bar and heads of a bar clamp.

26

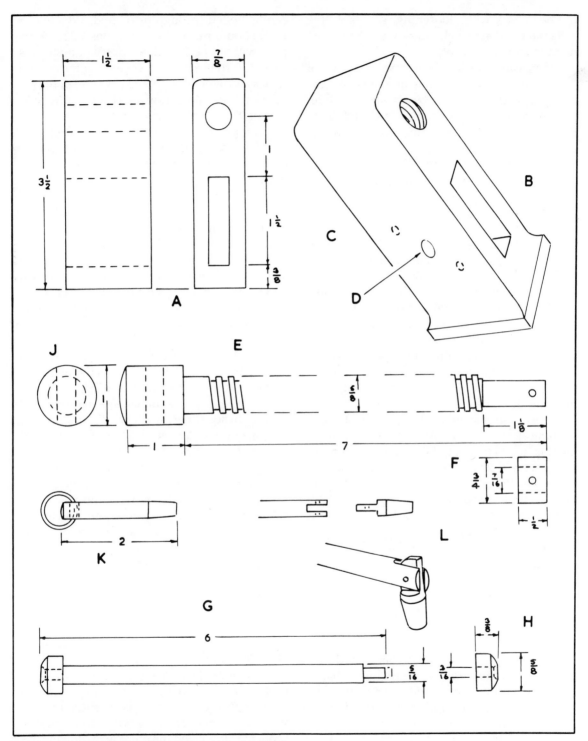

FIG. 6-3. Screw block (A-D), screw and pins (E-L).

27

the head back when loosening, so ensure the collar and end are level. Otherwise, there is no need for a precision fit.

If possible, make the screw a square or Acme thread, as a V thread would give too fine an adjustment and not be as strong under prolonged use. The thread need not go fully to the shoulder. Cut a matching thread through the block (FIG. 6-3A).

Make the lever from 5/16-inch rod (FIG. 6-3G). Make collars with domed tops (FIG. 6-3H) to fit on reduced ends so they can be riveted in position. Drill the head of the screw to allow the lever to slide easily (FIG. 6-3J).

The simplest pin is a piece of 3/8-inch rod, tapered throughout or just at the end (FIG. 6-3K). A ring through a hole allows it to be attached to the head with a cord or chain through a hole drilled in the head. If the end is made to swing down after fitting, it will reduce the risk of the pin coming out in use. Make a slot to take a lug and join the parts with a fine pin (FIG. 6-3L). Make the lug with one round corner and one square corner, then it should lock straight for pushing through a hole.

The clamp is shown with the movable head pushing against the pin. An alternative arrangement is to drill through the head so the pin can go through it. It will still be possible to put the pin behind the head, but on some occasions you may prefer it through.

The bar (FIG. 6-4A) should be checked for straightness in both planes. Square the ends. Drill holes to suit the peg at 2-inch intervals, starting 8 inches from the block end. Drill for rivets or bolts for the screw block. At the other end, drill and tap for a screw with a slotted head (FIG. 6-4B). This forms a stop to prevent the movable head from falling off, although it can be removed when you wish.

It is possible to extend the bar a moderate amount. You could keep a second longer bar to substitute for the normal one, or you can make an extension for another 24 inches or more. Prepare this with holes at 2-inch spacing, then add *cheeks*, or *fish plates*, on each side (FIG. 6-4C). They

can be bolted through or riveted. Whatever is used should make close fit in the holes, so the joint will not be forced out of true under pressure. Let the extending cheeks go far enough to miss the stop hole and take up two of the peg holes in the main bar, using closely fitting nuts and bolts.

For assembling many pieces of furniture, it is necessary to stand one or a pair of bar clamps on the bench top, ready for the assembled framing to be dropped in. Without help, it is easy to knock the clamps over as the wood parts are being located. That problem can be reduced if the bar clamps have feet. They should be arranged under the screw block and the movable head. There is no need to put them under the sliding head. If you use castings, the feet can be cast in and machined flat. If the parts are made from solid stock, suitable feet may be screwed on (FIG. 6-4D). They may be made from the same metal as the bar, 3/8-inch-by-1 1/2-inch and 5 inches long. Attach with two countersunk 5/16-inch screws, with their heads below the surface. Round all corners and edges.

Another problem in initial clamping is getting the heads square to the work. Additionally, the narrow steel heads tend to press into wood, so wood pads have to be used, making more things to hold when you are fully occupied getting the framework or carcase into place. The heads may be broadened with supplementary steel pads to aid squareness and spread the pressure (FIG. 6-4E). They can be 3/8-inch thick and as high as the normal pads. A suitable length would be 5 inches.

These pads could be drilled for screws and attached in the same way as the feet. Alternatively, put 3/8-inch square pieces to fit each side of the head, so the extra pads can be dropped into place or easily removed. These pieces could be welded, riveted, or screwed.

The normal use of a bar clamp is to squeeze parts together, usually to force joints tight. The force applied by the screw is considerable, and there are some occasions when this could be profitably employed the other way—forcing out-

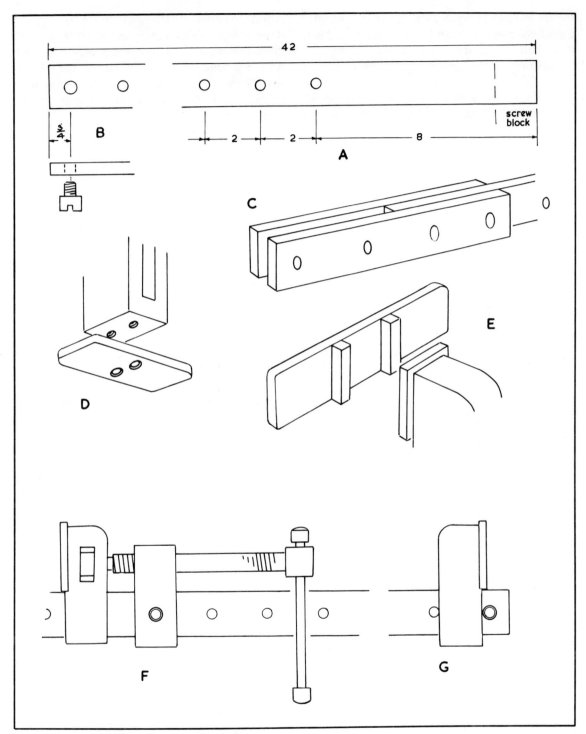

FIG. 6-4. Bar and clamping arrangements.

wards instead of squeezing inwards. The tool then becomes a jack and can be used to push boat parts into shape, force a frame tightly into an opening, or do other expanding or lifting work.

If the screw block is arranged to take off after releasing a bolt, it can be reversed and secured to one of the pin holes (FIG. 6-4F). Removing the stop screw at the other end allows the movable head to be taken off and turned around (FIG. 6-4G). When you turn the lever, do not make the end pieces thicker than specified, or they may not clear the bar when using the tool in this way.

7

Bench Shear

There is a limit to the thickness of sheet metal that can be cut by hand with snips, yet in many shops large shearing and cropping equipment may not be justified. Bench shears, operated by hand, work on the same scissors principle as snips, but the lever action produces considerable pressure and thick metal can be cut. What metals and thicknesses can be sheared depends on how substantially the bench shear is made, as well as the power you are able to apply to the lever.

This *bench shear* (FIG. 7-1) will cut sheet steel at least up to 1/8-inch thick and nonferrous metals slightly thicker. The length of cut is about 4 1/2 inches but, like snips, you can feed the cut across any width sheet. The tool is intended to bolt to a bench or stand. It covers a space 4-inches-by-12-inches and is 40 inches high with the lever up. The cut is 5 inches above the bench top. For greatest usefulness there should be an area all round to clear the largest sheet you expect to cut. There must also be enough space in front for the lever to be brought to horizontal.

The two blades are tool steel and should be hardened and tempered before use. The other parts may be mild steel. Many of the fastenings are ordinary nuts and bolts, but some have to be turned to also form pivots. It is important that the two blades slide over each other smoothly and with their meeting faces in the same plane. This means that the body should be assembled accurately, although set screws behind the lower blade will provide final adjustment.

The upper and lower body parts (FIG. 7-2A, B) are 1/2-inch or 5/8-inch plate. They have to be joggled so their inner surfaces are separated by a little more than the combined thicknesses of the blades. If suitable equipment is available, a single piece of steel may be given a double bend to make both parts. It is more likely that the two pieces will have to be joined with a spacer (FIG. 7-2C). For the strongest joint, this should be welded, but a sufficient depth is shown for bolting. The lever and links are simple strips with holes (FIG. 7-2D, E). The base of

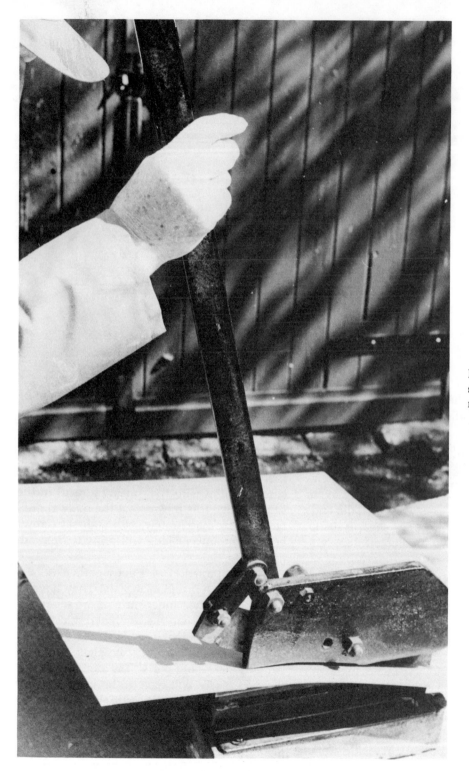

FIG. 7-1. A bench shear cuts sheet metal and rods.

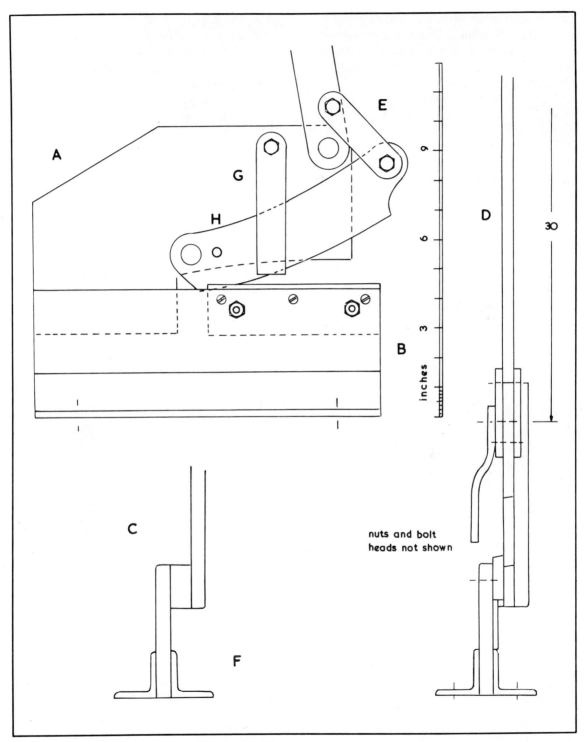

FIG. 7-2. General arrangements of the bench shear.

the shear is made of two pieces of angle steel (FIG. 7-2F), which could be welded or bolted on. Sheets are entered from the left, and a stop (FIG. 7-2G) prevents the metal from lifting under the shearing action.

The two blades should be of ground flat tool steel, 3/8-inch thick. Have the pieces available so the combined thickness can be measured. When assembled, the distance between the main parts should be about 0.015 inches more apart than the combined blade thickness, to allow adjustment. Check that the meeting faces of the body (FIG. 7-2A, B) are flat. Allow for the two parts overlapping by the size of the spacer (FIG. 7-3A). If the three pieces are to be welded, it need not be as deep as shown, but bolts or screws into tapped holes can be taken through the 1 1/2-inch depth drawn.

The bottom part of the body (FIG. 7-3B, C) is a parallel strip. The lower blade will stand 1/8 inch above it, but finish the edge straight. Its outer angle may be rounded. Mark the positions of the hexagonal-headed screws that will hold the lower blade and the three set screws that will provide adjustment (FIG. 7-3D), but do not drill the holes.

Make the top part of the body (FIG. 7-3E). Give the opening a moderate curve (FIG. 7-3F), to ensure adequate clearance and visibility for sheets being cut. The bevel at the back can be about the size shown, but it is only there to remove the sharp corner. Leave finishing the small bevel at the front (FIG. 7-3G) until assembly. It is about 45°, but one of the links has to close against it and act as a stop, so the lever finishes about 10° to vertical and is unlikely to fall forward accidentally. Mark the holes, but do not drill them.

Weld or screw the parts together. Make the two feet from angle steel. Sizes are not critical, but the angles shown are 1 1/2-inch-by-1 1/2-inch-by-3/16-inch (FIG. 7-3H).

With the steel for the blades annealed, cut them to shape and drill them. The bottom blade (FIG. 7-4A) is a plain rectangle. Drill it for 3/8-inch countersunk screws (FIG. 7-4B), so the heads go

below the surface.

The top blade has a curved cutting edge so it presents about the same cutting angle at all parts of the cut (FIG. 7-4C). Drill a 1/2-inch hole for the pivot (FIG. 7-4D) and a 3/8-inch hole for the bolt through the links.

The cutting angle of the edges need only be slight—7° is suggested (FIG. 7-4E). Grind both blades to this angle, then harden and temper them.

Drill the holes in the body to take the bottom blade. The three adjusting set screws can be 1/4 inch or 5/16 inch. Drill and thread their holes to match (FIG. 7-4F).

Make the handle (FIG. 7-4G). At the lower end, drill to fit a similar pivot to the top blade (FIG. 7-4D) and round the end. The 3/8-inch hole for the links is towards one edge (FIG. 7-4H) to ensure the links have enough clearance in use. At the other end, round the edges as well as the top to make a comfortable grip. Make two links (FIG. 7-4J) with 3/8-inch holes for bolts.

The stop (FIG. 7-2G) is held by a single bolt so it can be swung out of the way when not needed. So it holds at a reasonable distance from the cutting edge, give it a double bend (FIG. 7-4K). At the top, make a collar (FIG. 7-4L) to hold the stop away from the body.

Make two pivots (FIG. 7-4D). The shouldered part (FIG. 7-4M) has to match the part that fits on it. For the handle, there can be an easy fit, but for the top blade there should not be much play, so the blade moves without wobbling. Having the length of the shouldered part not more than 0.015 inch greater than the blade thickness should be satisfactory.

Attach the handle by its pivot and a nut to the body. Fit the top blade by its pivot and a nut in the same way. Join the two with links on each side and bolts. Move the lever so you can see how much to take off the corner (FIG. 7-3G) for the lever to swing back about 10° to vertical, or enough to prevent it falling forward accidentally. Put lock nuts on the bolts through the links, either double nuts or other locking types.

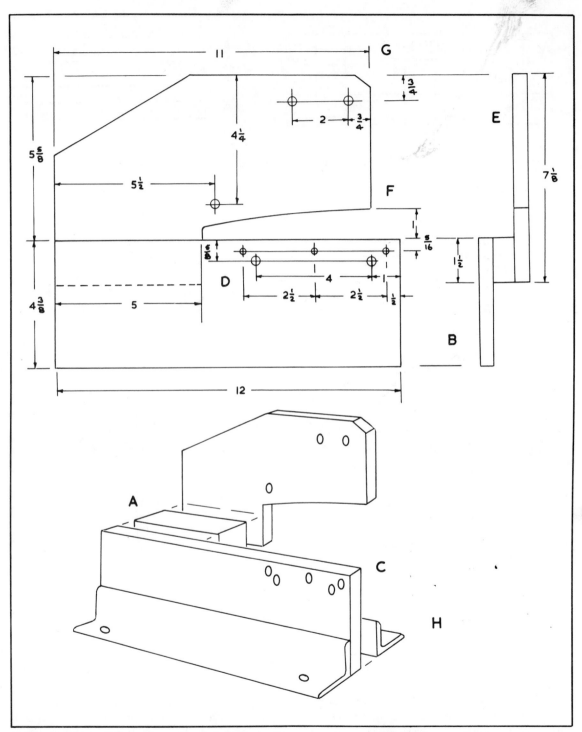

FIG. 7-3. Sizes of the main parts of the bench shear.

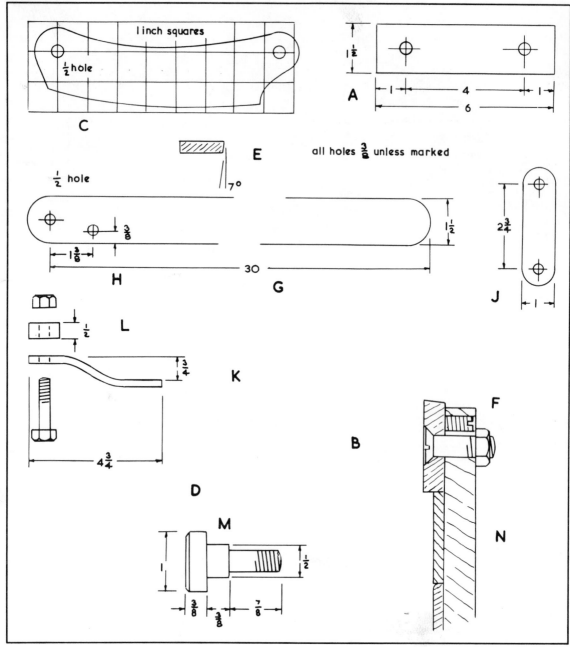

FIG. 7-4. Moving parts of the bench shear.

Try the action of the blades over each other. By slacking the lower blade holding screws and tightening the set screws, or the other way, adjust the bottom blade (FIG. 7-4B, F) so it bears closely against the top blade throughout a cut.

To relieve the fixing screws of some of the considerable load when the machine is cutting, it is advisable to put a support piece between the blade and the top edge of the angle forming a foot (FIG. 7-4N). It can be held in place with tapped screws or small bolts taken through.

Mount the top in position and bolt down the shear so it can be tested. Some lubrication of moving parts is advisable at first, but should be unnecessary in later use.

It is possible to modify the machine to chop off rod, but it is inadvisable to consider anything thicker than 5/16-inch diameter, whatever the metal. After making the top blade, but before hardening and tempering it, mount it in the raised position. Drill a 3/8-inch hole through the body and blade (FIG. 7-2H). Keeping it fairly close to the pivot ensures maximum leverage. Harden and temper the blade. Nothing can be done to harden the mild steel body, so in use, the edge of the hole in the body will wear rounded and efficiency in cutting rods will get lower, but this facility can be expected to remain workable for some time.

8

Miter Clamps

A picture framer needs to be able to pull corner joints tight and hold them while the glue sets. Usually, the miters are simple cuts and there are no dowels or tenons to interlock and provide strength, but in most frames there are thin nails driven one or both ways. There should be space for nails to be driven while the mitered corner is in the clamp.

There are two ways that picture frame molding can be held in a corner clamp. Pressure can be applied from the inside outwards by a central screw, or it can be applied inwards with two screws. Both methods are satisfactory and have advantages in certain circumstances. The single screw pushing outwards suits narrow molding, while the two-screw type has a better capacity for larger and ornate moldings. Examples of both types are described here, in sizes that should suit most types of picture frames. Of course, they would suit other mitered assemblies as well. Even if only light moldings are to be clamped, it is inadvisable to reduce the sizes of parts of the clamps. They must remain rigid

under pressure, and weight is an advantage when driving nails.

Single-screw Miter Clamp

This clamp (FIG. 8-1A) has a base of 1/4-inch steel plate, with shaped turned pieces supporting the molding and a screw through a hexagonal block applying pressure to a piece that goes into the rabbets of the moldings (FIG. 8-2A). The parts are mounted on the base, with domed nuts underneath forming feet (FIG. 8-2B).

Make the base (FIG. 8-2C). Squareness between the three outer holes is most important. The other hole is on a line 45° to them. The holes are 1/2 inch, and the corners are 3/4-inch radius around them. Slightly round all edges for comfort in handling.

The pressure piece (FIG. 8-2D) is 1 3/4-inch square and 1-inch thick. It is cut down so the edges press inside the molding rabbet (FIG. 8-2E) and not on the edge, which could be damaged. Most rabbets are more than 1/2-inch deep, and that is the thickness allowed for the pressing

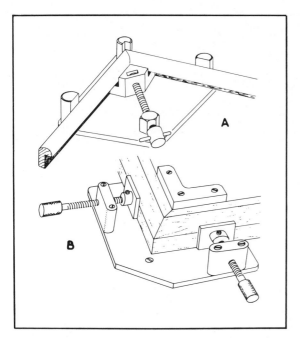

FIG. 8-1. A single-screw miter clamp (A), which tightens outwards and a two-screw miter clamp tightening inwards (B).

edge. It could be made thinner, but there would then be a risk of pressing excessively into the wood. With shallower rabbets, it would be better to put a thin packing under the molding.

Make sure the edges of the pressure piece are square. After cutting the rabbet, take off the corner as shown (FIG. 8-2F). The edges that will meet the wood may be left plain, but pressure toward the corner will be increased and slipping reduced if they are given teeth (FIG. 8-2G). Leave cutting the slot until the screw is made.

The three pieces that support the molding are turned from 1-inch diameter rod, reduced to 1/2-inch to go through the base and screw into the nuts. The two outer pieces (FIG. 8-3A) have flats on them, taken back to the reduced diameter (FIG. 8-3B). Make the corner piece the same size, but cut a 90° groove in it (FIG. 8-3C), taken in to the reduced diameter (FIG. 8-3D), which should bring its faces in line with the flats on the other posts when they are mounted.

Make four domed nuts (FIG. 8-3E) from

1-inch hexagonal bar. Drill to take the ends of the posts, and screw these parts sufficiently to tighten on the base.

The other post could also be made from round rod, but it is shown made from 1-inch hexagonal bar (FIG. 8-3F), reduced at the end the same as the other pieces (FIG. 8-3G).

The screw is made from 3/4-inch rod reduced to 3/8-inch (FIG. 8-3H). The length shown will allow the clamp to take molding from under 1/2 inch to over 1 1/2 inches. At the large end, drill across for a 1/4-inch diamter rod (FIG. 8-3J). Reduce the end to take a collar (FIG. 8-3K), which will be held in place with a pin. Cut a coarse thread on the screw and a matching hole in the hexagonal post (FIG. 8-3G).

The hole and slot in the pressure piece (FIG. 8-2H) take the end of the screw and its collar. Pass the screw through its post, then take the reduced end into the slot and secure the collar with its pin. Use a square to check that the matching faces of posts A and D are true, then mount the hexagonal post. Check that the screw is at 45° and the pressure piece is exactly central. Test with pieces of molding.

Two-screw Miter Clamp

This clamp tightens from the outside and has a capacity for up to 3-inch moldings. It is shown with screws having knurled knobs (FIG. 8-1B), but they could have pins through or be given other types of grip. The parts are bolted to a base with domed nuts, which form feet, in a similar way to the other miter clamp. All of the parts are mild steel. The two screws are directed at the center of the L-shaped black (FIG. 8-4A). If sizes are altered, arrange these parts in the same manner.

Make the base (FIG. 8-4B). The positions of the holes are best marked from the parts that fit over them. Corners should be rounded to match them. All parts are joined with 3/8-inch screws.

The two screw blocks are the same (FIG. 8-4C), drilled and countersunk for the fixing screws, and with the ends rounded (FIG. 8-4D).

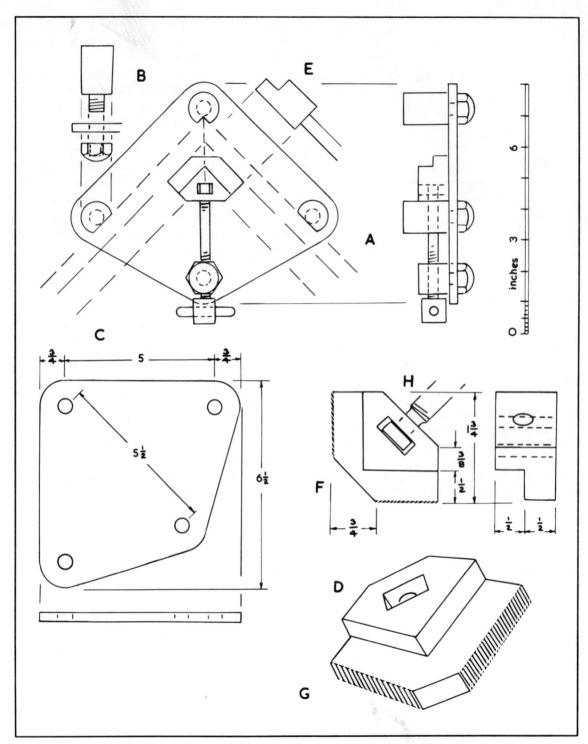

FIG. 8-2. Sizes and details of the main parts of a single-screw miter clamp.

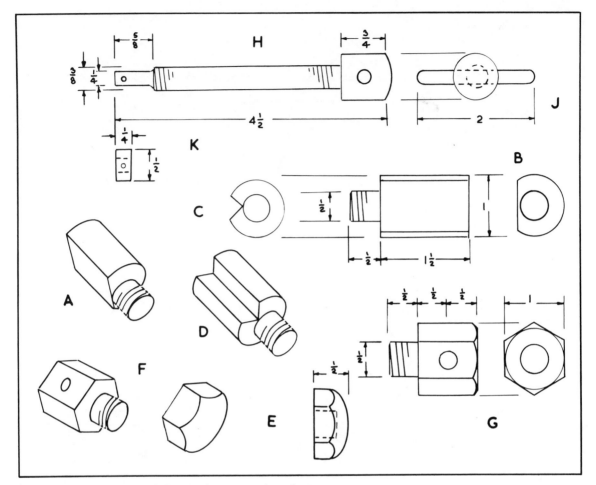

FIG. 8-3. Turned parts of the single-screw miter clamp.

Leave drilling the tightening screw holes until those screws are made.

Make the screws from 7/8-inch rod reduced to 7/16-inch diameter (FIG. 8-5A). Round the end and knurl the large part to provide a grip. The tip has to fit into the pressure pad, where it is held with a screw (FIG. 8-5B). Reduce the end and make a groove 1/8 inch wide to take the securing screw. Cut a coarse thread for the full length of the 7/16-inch diameter parts and make a thread through each screw block to match.

The pressure pads (FIG. 8-5C) are rectangular with central bosses. They could be turned from solid stock, built up by brazing, or made from castings. Leave a small curved fillet be-

tween the bosses and the flat part. Drill centrally to take the end of the tightening screws (FIG. 8-5D). Check that the outline is square both ways and the hole for the end of the screw is the same height as that in the screw blocks.

Drill into the bosses for a securing screw (FIG. 8-5E). This could be 3/16-inch diameter with its end reduced to suit the groove in the tightening screw end.

Make the L-shaped block 1 1/2 inches high (FIG. 8-5F). Drill for three fixing screws and round the outside, with the end holes as centers. Shape the inside to a similar curve (FIG. 8-5G). Make a small bevel across the corner, to be clear of any ragged wood edges or escaping glue.

41

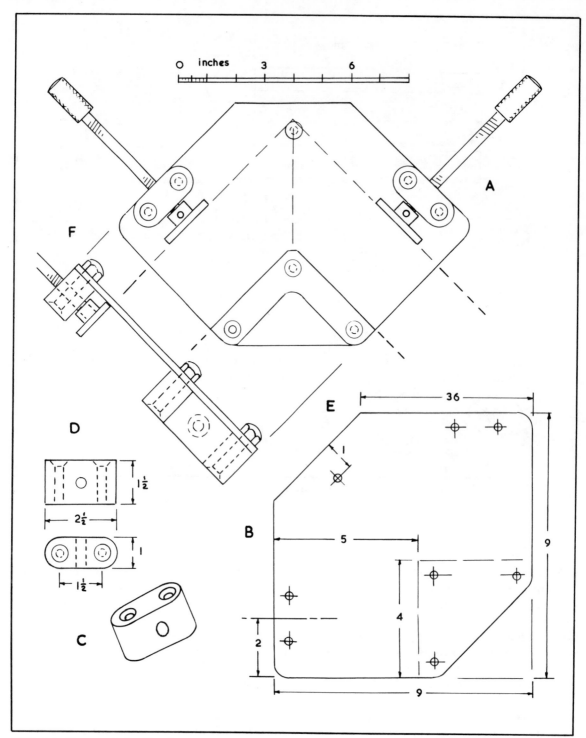

FIG. 8-4. Sizes and details of a two-screw miter clamp.

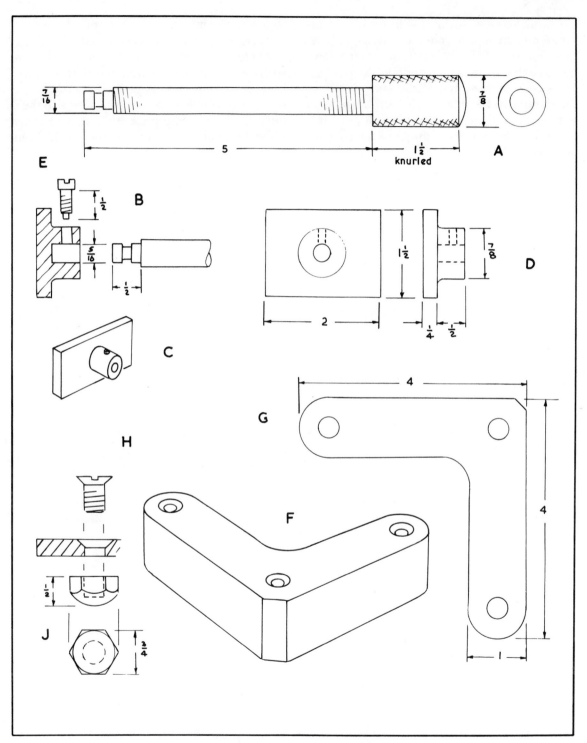

FIG. 8-5. Sizes of the clamping parts of the two-screw miter clamp.

So the base will stand without tilting, arrange a countersunk screw through (FIG. 8-4E) near the edge. This (FIG. 8-5H) and other screws go through to domed nuts underneath (FIG. 8-5J). Make eight of these nuts all the same depth, so the clamp will stand firm (FIG. 8-3F). If you wish to fasten the clamp down to a bench or board, substitute plain collars of the same depth, with holes right through in at least three positions, so longer screws can be taken into the wood.

Countersink for all screws so the heads go just below the surface. Cut the screws to length so they will tighten within the domed nuts. Round exposed corners of the base.

First assemble with the screws loose in their nuts. Check that the pressure pads will come squarely against the faces of the block, then tighten all screws to the base.

9

Sawing Guide

Picture frame miters have to be cut accurately if the frame is to look right and one or more gaping joints are not to spoil appearance. The miter arrangements on most table saws are not very accurate, and even a fine circular saw will leave a surface too rough for use as it is. Picture framers prefer to cut their miters in moldings by hand with a fine backsaw. The slower cut and fine teeth will leave a miter that may need no further treatment. The problem is guiding the saw so the cut is accurate.

There are many miter saw guides, from simple notched pieces of wood to elaborate machines. This *saw guide* (FIG. 9-1) is simple to use and will control a backsaw at any set angle. Besides 45° for a square corner, 30° is needed for a hexagonal frame, and 22 1/2° for an octagonal one. The guide can also be set to 90°. Molding should rest on a thin wood packing. Plastic inserts in the guide posts prevent the saw teeth coming into contact with metal.

All of the parts may be made of mild steel, but aluminum alloy would make a lighter guide.

The posts and screws may be brass. The guide has feet at the ends; a strip of wood bolted to them would allow the guide to be gripped in a vise (FIG. 9-2A). The arm that controls the angle of cut swings under the base and can be locked at any position with a screw (FIG. 9-2B). Molding is held by hand or with clamps against the upright pieces (FIG. 9-2C).

Lay out the base (FIG. 9-3A) on 3/8-inch or 1/2-inch plate. The key positions are the center of the post (FIG. 9-3B) and the line of the upright pieces. With a line through the post center square to the line of the uprights, mark the positions of the locating screw holes (FIG. 9-3C). The holes at the end are for the feet. Cut the outline.

Make and attach the upright pieces. They may be welded on or screws may be driven upwards from underneath. Check squareness to the base.

Make the arm from 3/8-inch or 1/2-inch bar (FIG. 9-3D). Leave drilling the holes in this and the base until the other parts have been prepared.

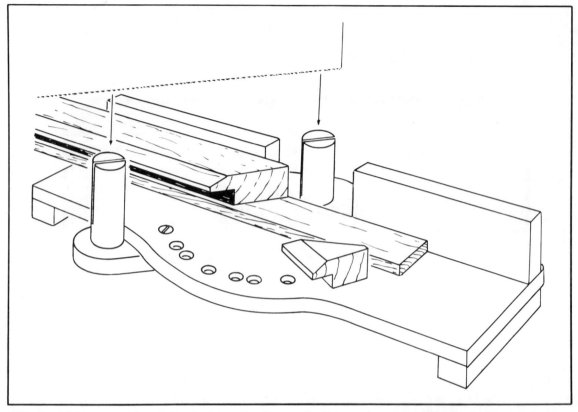

FIG. 9-1. This saw guide can be used to cut miters and other angles on moldings or strip wood.

The two posts are made from 1-inch diameter rod. The one on the arm is longer by the thickness of the base (FIG. 9-3E). Make the pivot post (FIG. 9-3F) with a shouldered end reduced to 5/8-inch diameter and of a length to pass through the base and still allow enough clearance for movement when it is tightly screwed to the arm (FIG. 9-3G). Drill the base to suit. Drill and tap a hole to take a 3/8-inch screw in both posts. Make screws with shallow hexagonal heads to fit over washers and hold the posts. Drill the arm to suit.

For the saw guides, make slots 3/8-inch wide (FIG. 9-3H) to within 1/8 inch of the base level. Use epoxy adhesive to fit in nylon or other plastic strips. Cut down the centers, either with the saw that will be used for cutting wood or another of the same thickness, to within 1/8 inch

of the bottom of the plastic (FIG. 9-3J). When moldings are being cut, have a piece of wood at least 3/8-inch thick under them, so the saw teeth do not touch the metal base, nor saw the plastic deeper.

Drill for the locating screw with countersunk clearance holes in the base (FIG. 9-2D). Arrange for the screw head to be below the surface and to tighten into a tapped hole in the arm. Test the action of the arm with the posts attached and check angles.

Make the feet 1-inch wide and deep enough to keep the screw heads in the arm above the bench (FIG. 9-2E). Attach them with countersunk screws. If you want to, hold the guide in a vise drill and tap the feet to take screws holding a strip of wood (FIG. 9-2A).

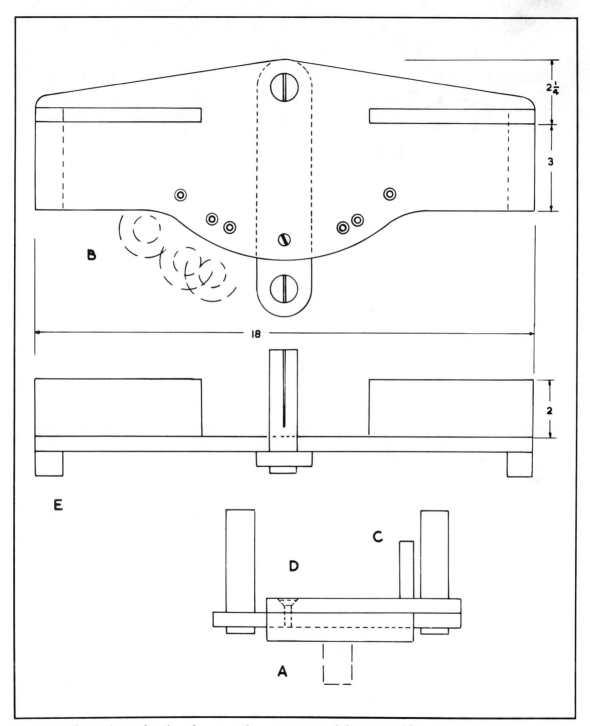

FIG. 9-2. Three views showing the general arrangement of the saw guide.

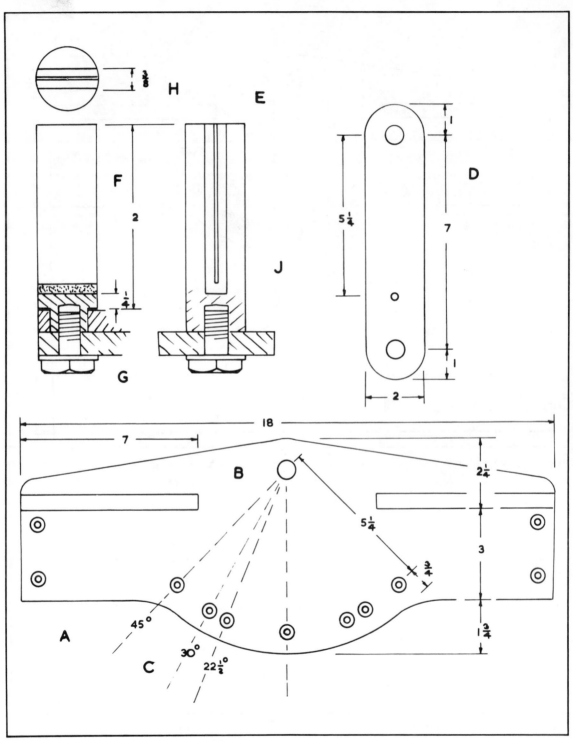

FIG. 9-3. Sizes of parts of the saw guide.

10
Lathe Screw Chuck

In wood turning, if the wood is not spindle-shaped to mount between centers, it has to be supported only at the headstock end. Large bowls are mounted on a faceplate, but smaller items, like eggcups, pin bowels, and chess men, are unsuitable for holding with screws through holes in a faceplate. They are better held with a pad like a small faceplate, but with a projecting central screw.

Some lathes are provided with screw chucks in which the screw is an integral part and cannot be replaced, so when the threads become worn and they do not grip the wood, the whole fitting becomes useless. This screw center (FIG. 10-1) takes an ordinary wood screw, which can be removed. Besides allowing a replacement, this permits screws of different lengths to be used. If the wood beds closely against the face of the chuck, the screw has a strong grip and is unlikely to slip in end grain. If the article being turned is larger than the chuck, additional screws can be driven through holes near its rim.

This screw chuck (FIG. 10-2A) may be threaded to fit on the lathe mandrel nose. If the lathe has a self-centering chuck, the screw chuck can be gripped in it. So the lathe tools do not touch the metal, a pad of plywood or hardboard may be put on the screw (FIG. 10-2B), leaving enough of it projecting to grip the wood.

All parts are mild steel. Size will depend on the lathe mandrel. The chuck shown is intended for a 7/8-inch diameter mandrel. The overall diameter of 2 3/4 inches should support wood up to the diameter requiring a faceplate. The steel wood screw size chosen should be fairly thick. That shown has a neck diameter of 1/4 inch. A length of 1 inch will suit most jobs, but the wood turner may wish to keep available screws of the same gauge, but of different lengths.

Turn the outside to size (FIG. 10-2C). The rim may be knurled to provide a grip when fitting and removing the chuck, but the action of turning will tighten the chuck and leverage will be needed to remove it. Drill a hole (FIG. 10-2D) in the rim so a piece of 1/4-inch rod can be inserted

FIG. 10-1. A screw center or chuck is used to hold small pieces being turned in a wood lathe.

to use as a lever. Two or four holes (FIG. 10-2E) can be drilled so additional screws may be driven.

Bore and screw to fit the mandrel nose (FIG. 10-2F). If there is a shoulder on the mandrel make the length of the chuck suitable to bear against it, so the turning load is not taken by the screw thread only.

On the face of the chuck, there is a screwed hollow to take two inserts that hold the wood screw. The first insert (FIG. 10-2G) goes to the bottom of the hollow and carries a key which engages with the wood screw slot (FIG. 10-2H). The other insert holds the screw (FIG. 10-2J) and presses it down on the key (FIG. 10-2K).

As drawn, the hollow is 3/4-inch diameter and 3/4-inch deep, but it may be modified to suit your wood screw and equipment. It could be made deeper and shouldered for convenience in screwing. Cut a fine thread inside, to match that to be used on the inserts.

Make the first insert to screw to the bottom or shoulder of the recess. The key (FIG. 10-2L) does not have to make a tight fit in the wood screw slot. It only provides drive, not grip. It should, however, be a push fit in the slot in the insert, so it does not fall out when the chuck is opened. When the key is tight against the bottom of the slot in its insert, it should not reach the bottom of the slot in the screw head when the screw head is tight against the insert. It is unlikely that this insert will have to be removed again, so use the slot for a screwdriver and drive it in tightly.

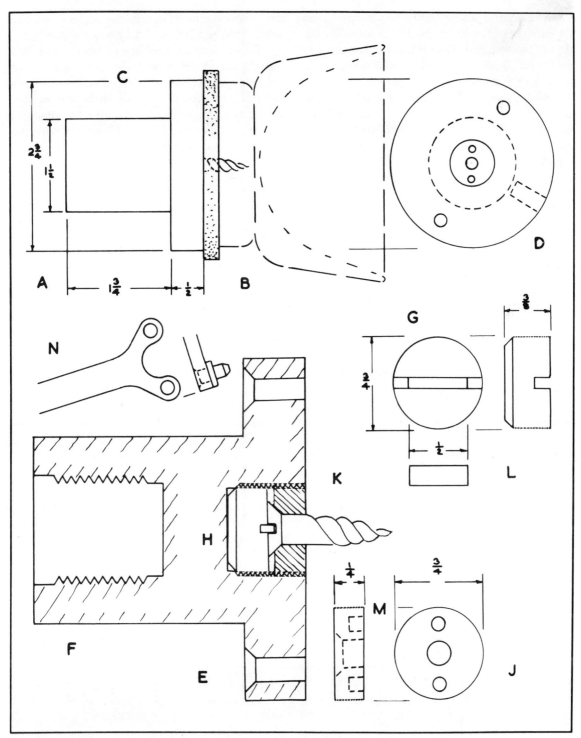

FIG. 10-2. Sizes of a screw chuck that contains a replaceable wood screw.

The second insert has to finish flush with the surface of the chuck body, so make it a little too thick at first. Drill it for the wood screw and countersink it so about half the depth of the head remains above the surface.

So the insert can be tightened or loosened, drill two holes (FIG. 10-2M). The insert could be rotated with a punch, but it is better to make a tool to fit in the holes (FIG. 10-2N). This may be 1/8-inch thick and 3 inches long, shaped to clear the screw center. Pegs in the forked end are taken through holes and lightly riveted.

Fit the wood screw head onto the key and tighten the insert onto it. Level the surface of the insert with the surrounding surface. It does not matter if the insert is slightly below the surface of the chuck body, but it should not stand above it, because that would interfere with the larger surface providing drive.

11

Combination Square Additions

The *combination square* is a versatile tool, with its square and miter head usually containing a *level* and a *scriber*. If it has *protractor* and *center* heads, its scope is increased, and it always includes a graduated *straightedge* or *rule*. In its most refined form, it is a tool for the precision metalworker, while in its less advanced form it is something to take the place of several individual tools for other craftsmen, including the many types of woodworkers.

It is possible to increase its versatility for any of these craftsmen by making other parts to fit on it. Some of these can make the basic square into calipers, height gauge, trammels or compass, and scribing block (FIG. 11-1).

Calipers

An extra sliding head mounted square to the rule can be used with the normal square head as calipers, having a greater reach than on the usual sliding calipers, making the arrangement suitable for use on diameters of up to 7 inches when turning metal or wood (FIG. 11-1A), if mounted on the usual 12-inch rule.

Sizes of the new head will depend on the actual dimensions of the combination square, but those suggested suit the common type with a rule 3/32-inch thick and 1-inch wide, and the square head projecting 3 1/2 inches.

Make the caliper head (FIG. 11-2A) from 3/4-inch-by-1-inch steel. The length from the bottom of the slot should be the same as that below the slot on the square and miter head. The head is locked to the rule in a very similar way, but the screw projects above the rule. True the ends of the bar and drill down a central hole to clear a 3/16-inch screwed rod. Across this, cut a slot to slide on the rule (FIG. 11-2B), with no more clearance than necessary for ease of working.

Below the slot, reduce the blade to 1/4-inch thick (FIG. 11-2C). Remove sharpness of edges, but otherwise leave the blade square.

The screw that locks the caliper head to the rule has a similar form to that holding the ex-

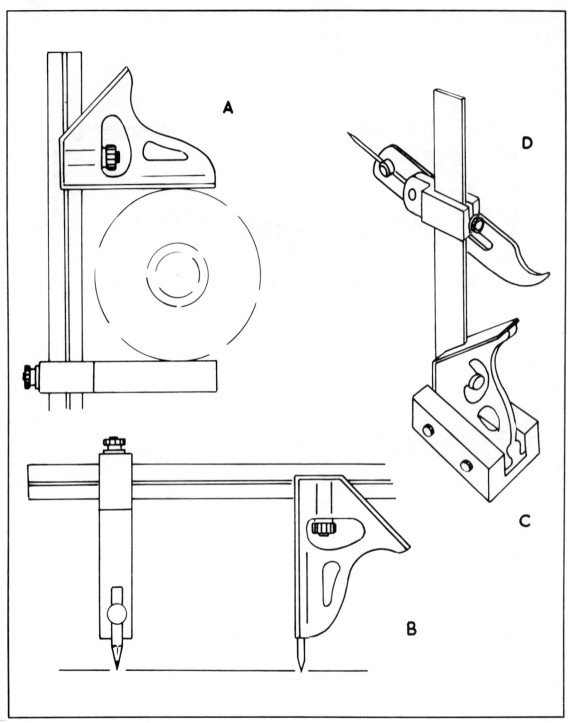

FIG. 11-1. Extra parts on a combination square allow it to be used as calipers (A), a compass (B), or a height gauge or scribing block (C-D).

isting heads. Remove one of these screws and compare sizes. The screw is a piece of 3/16-inch rod, reduced to fit one side of the rule; a projection on the end fits loosely in the rule slot (FIG. 11-2D). Cut this part long enough to clear the width of the rule.

Make a knurled nut (FIG. 11-2E) to the sizes shown or to match those on other heads. Below this comes a washer, and the rod is threaded far enough for the nut to pull the caliper head tight against the rule. The top edges and corners of the head may be rounded.

Trammels

With the caliper head, it is possible to make the combination square into trammels or a beam compass, suitable for any radius up to about 10 inches on a 12-inch rule (FIG. 11-1B).

If the square and miter head has a scriber pushed into its end, use the same hole for the point of the compass. If your square is without a scriber hole, drill a small hole at the end of the head, square to the line of the rule. It need not be deeper than 3/8 inch and could be 1/8-inch diameter. Make a piece from round tool steel to press into the hole and project about 1/2 inch with a needle point. It should be possible to fit and remove the point with pliers. If the hole is continued with a smaller drill, it should be possible to reverse the point when out of use and store it in the head.

If the tool will be used only as trammels with a scribing point, the caliper head can be arranged to take another needle point. A wood-

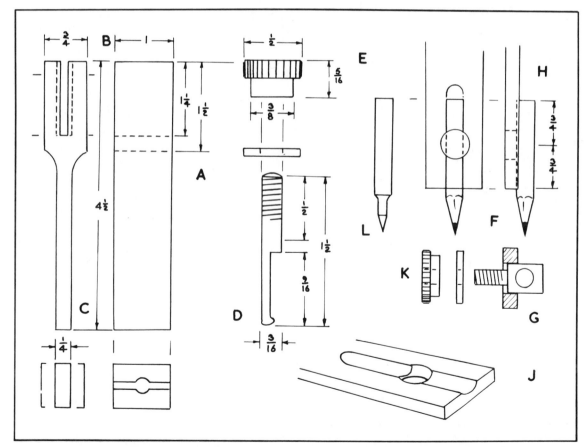

FIG. 11-2. Sizes and details of the caliper and compass arms for attaching to a combination square.

worker will want to use a pencil as well, and the modification is shown to suit that (FIG. 11-2F).

The pencil is held by a 1/2-inch screwed rod. Drill it across to take a piece of an ordinary wood pencil (FIG. 11-2G). (It might also take a ball-point pen.) Drill the caliper head to take the rod (FIG. 11-2H) and put a shallow groove in it to position the pencil (FIG. 11-2J).

Turn down the rod to 1/4 inch, far enough for the larger diameter to be within the thickness of the head when the screw is tightened. Make a knurled nut and washer to draw the pencil into the groove.

If the head is only required to take a point, for use as dividers or trammels, make a 1/8-inch tool steel rod with a point, and make the clamping arrangement and groove to suit that. If the tool is to be used with a pencil or a scribing point, make a tool steel part the same diameter as a pencil, but reduced and pointed at the end (FIG. 11-2L).

Base

There are occasions when you need to stand the tool on the flat face of the square and miter head, as when you need to check an internal 90°, or use the level to check a surface, or use the rule with it to test that a part is vertical or plumb. The face of the head does not offer a very big or steady area of contact. Most heads

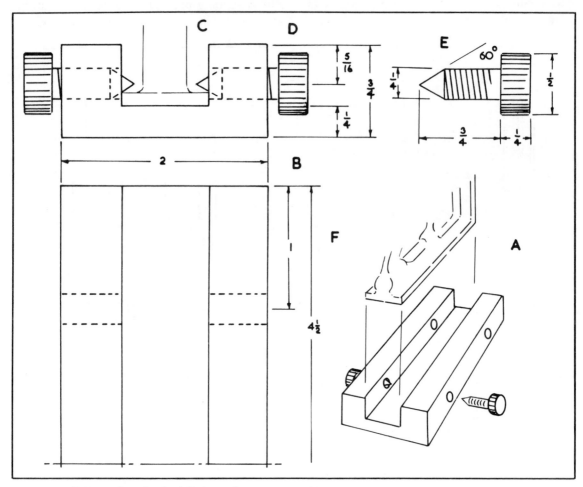

FIG. 11-3. Sizes and method of fitting a base to a combination square.

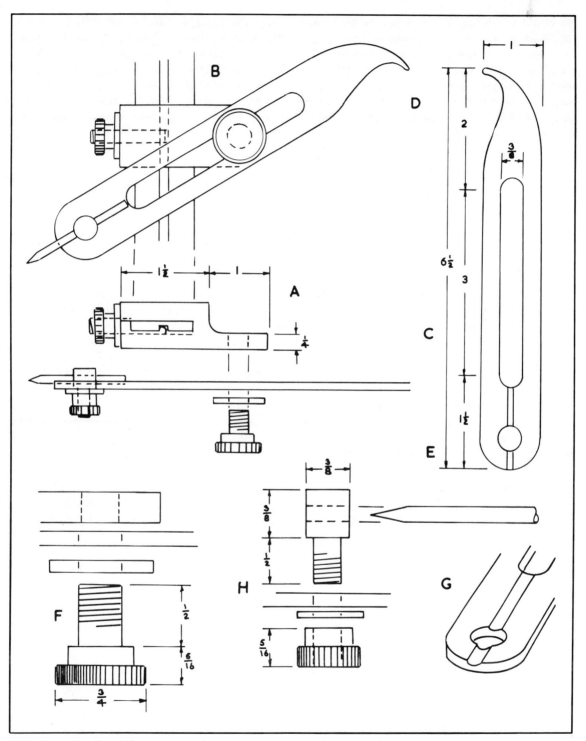

FIG. 11-4. Details of the parts required to convert a combination square to a height gauge.

are about 3/4 inch by 4 inches. It is better to increase the area by an additional base (FIG. 11-1C). This also makes the square more suitable for adapting as a height gauge or scribing block, where the broad heavy base is an advantage. Sizes may have to be modified, but those shown suit a head 3/4-inch wide and 4 inches long, with the rule extending a further 1/4 inch. The rim that has to be gripped is under 1/8-inch thick (FIG. 11-3A).

The base is 3/4-inch thick, 2 inches wide, and 4 1/2 inches long, machined flat all around (FIG. 11-3B). Cut a groove parallel with the under surface to match the width of the square head (FIG. 11-3C).

Screws have to be arranged at a height that allows their pointed ends to grip the inner surfaces of the head. Check the edge thickness and clearance inside the head around the level casing and the web. The arrangement drawn should suit most square heads (FIG. 11-3D).

The screws are 1/4-inch diameter, with knurled heads and points at 60° (FIG. 11-3E). Check the distance apart for holes to suit your square, but 1 inch from each end will suit most squares (FIG. 11-3F). Tap the holes to suit the screws. The entrances to the holes may be clearance size, and only about half the depth needs to be threaded.

When the base is assembled for use, the end under the rule should not project past that edge, so it does not interfere with *dealing* with an internal angle.

Height Gauge

If the combination square is mounted on its base, the upright rule can support an arm to measure or compare heights. If it is reversed, its scribing point makes it suitable for marking heights as the tool is drawn along a surface plate or other flat surface (FIG. 11-1D).

Many sizes of arm are possible, but that drawn (FIG. 11-4) should suit most purposes. The attachment is similar to the top part of the caliper head, and the arm can be made from a 1/8-inch-by-1-inch strip.

Make the support from 3/4-inch-by-1-inch steel (FIG. 11-4A, B), and make the slot and attachment parts the same as those for the caliper head (FIG. 11-2, A-E). Reduce the projecting part to 1/4-inch thick. Mark the center of the hole and round the end.

Make the arm (FIG. 11-4C) with a 3/8-inch slot. Shape the tip to make a feeler (FIG. 11-4D). Mark the center of the hole at the other end and round the outside (FIG. 11-4E).

For attaching the arm to the support, make a knurled screw with 3/8-inch diameter thread to pass through a washer and the slotted arm into a tapped hole in the support (FIG. 11-4F).

To hold the scriber point, drill a 3/8-inch hole and make a groove to locate the 1/8-inch diameter scriber (FIG. 11-4G). Make the scriber holder from 3/8-inch diameter rod, reduced to 1/4-inch for screwing. When the scriber is in position, the end of the 3/8-inch diameter part should be within the thickness of the arm, so tightening the knurled nut over its washer pulls the scriber tight into its slot. Make the hardened and tempered scriber so it projects about 1/2 inch when its body fills most of the slot in the arm.

12

Blocks and Tackle

One of the simplest ways of gaining a mechanical advantage is to use an arrangement of ropes and pulleys. In theory, almost any advantage can be gained by using enough pulleys, but there are practical limitations, notably the amount of rope to be pulled through. For instance, with a mechanical advantage of 12:1, the tackle has to be set up with a considerable length of rope and for every 1 foot moved by the load, 12 feet of rope has to be pulled through.

Traditional rope users call the pulleys *sheaves* and pronounce the word "*shivs*." The arrangement of rope and blocks is *tackle* pronounced "*tayckle*." With any arrangement of blocks, it is possible to alter the mechanical advantage by reversing the tackle, said to "rig to advantage" for the greater pull or to "rig to disadvantage" the other way.

The mechanical advantage is identified by counting the number of lines coming from the moving block. With two single blocks (one without the rope end attached) joined to the load and the other fixed, the advantage is 2:1 (FIG. 12-1A). If the arrangement is reversed, there are three lines from the moving block and the advantage is 3:1 (FIG. 12-1B). There are losses due to friction, but they need not be very great.

Tackle made up of a single and a double block is useful for general purposes, giving mechanical advantages of 3:1 or 4:1. This is sufficient for hauling a boat up a ramp or lifting a car engine (FIG. 12-1C).

Modern synthetic fiber rope is very strong, and thin rope may have adequate strength. It needs to be thick enough for comfortable handling, however, so 1/2-inch diameter rope is suggested as the minimum size for which blocks should be made.

The blocks described here have plain bearings with arrangements for lubrication, but the wheels may be fitted with ball or roller bearings. Much of any friction loss in tackle is internal, in the bending rope, and this is reduced by avoiding making the sheaves of two small diameter. The blocks may be made of mild steel;

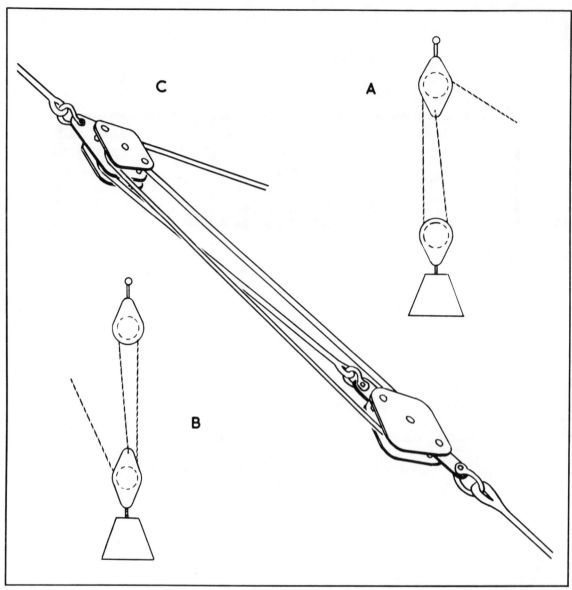

FIG. 12-1. The mechanical advantage of rope tackle can be identified by the number of lines coming from the moving block—2:1 (A) or 3:1 (B). Advantage is increased by using a double with a single block (C).

for regular use near salt water they would be better made of bronze.

Single Block

The block has two cheeks extending on each side of the sheave and with extensions on both ends of the shackles or other arrangements for attaching ropes (FIG. 12-2). The sizes shown are intended for 1/2-inch diameter fiber rope.

Make the sheave first (FIG. 12-2A, B). The boss is 1-inch diameter and the sides are turned 1/16 inch narrower on each side. At the rim, the groove has some clearance on the rope in its width and is made deeper than semicircular, to

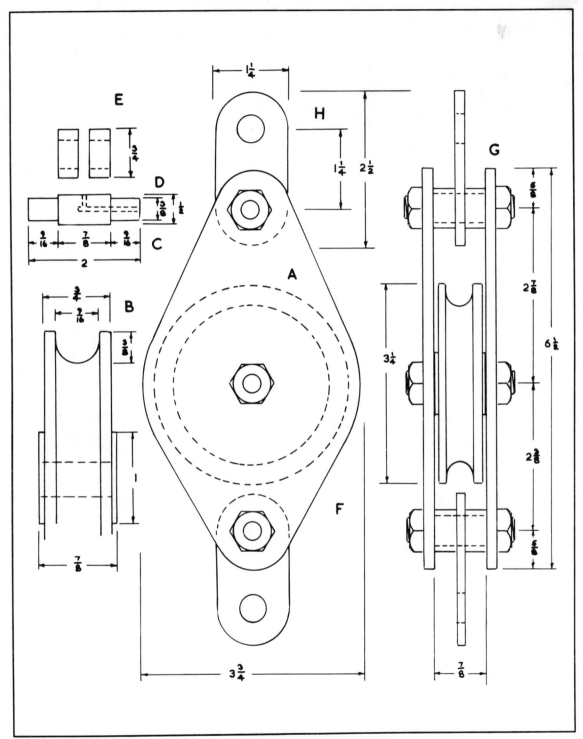

FIG. 12-2. Sizes and construction of a single block.

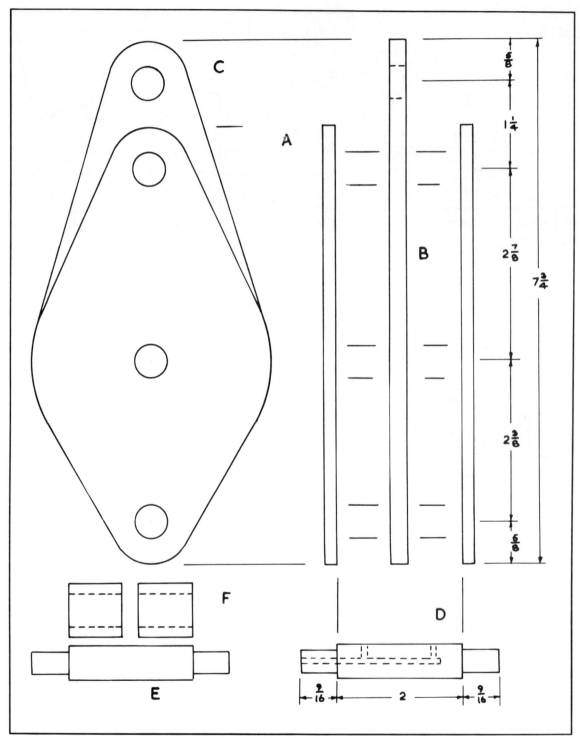

FIG. 12-3. Arrangement of parts of a double block.

aid in retaining the rope when slack. Take sharpness off the edges. Drill a 1/2 inch hole.

The axle and the two spacers are the same size (FIG. 12-2C). The distance between shoulders should be enough to give working clearance to the boss of the sheave. The reduced ends will be screwed to take nuts, which may be thin locknuts. Allow enough length to pass through the cheeks and nuts and extend about 1/16 inch.

Make an oil passage in the axle by drilling a 3/32-inch hole centrally and another into it (FIG. 12-2D). In use, the block can be put on its side and oil introduced from a can, or you can fit a nipple to connect with a grease gun.

At the ends, the extensions are kept central by two collars on the spacers (FIG. 12-2E). They could be pieces of tube or turned from rod.

The two cheeks are the same (FIG. 12-2F, G) and made from 3/16-inch plate. Mark out from a centerline and draw the curves about the hole centers before drilling them 3/8-inch diameter. Smooth and slightly round the edges to avoid risk of damaging the rope.

The extensions (FIG. 12-2H) are also 3/16-inch plate. Drill to fit on the spacers. It is usual to attach rope with shackles, which are loops with screws across the ends. Holes of 3/8-inch or 1/2-inch diameter should match a suitable shackle.

Assemble the parts with an initial coating of grease on the axle. The sheave should turn easily and may need its thickness reduced slightly for a smooth action. Tighten all nuts. It may be advisable to lightly rivet the extending ends to prevent nuts coming off.

Double Block

In a block with two sheaves, the central plate can project to take the place of the extensions in the single block. Unless you intend to use the double block in more elaborate tackle, there is no need to make provision for a shackle at the bottom of the block (FIG. 12-3). Many of the details of the double block are the same as its single partner.

Make two sheaves the same as for the single block. The two cheeks are also the same (FIG. 12-3A).

The central dividing piece (FIG. 12-3B) should be increased to 1/4-inch thick. Its lower part matches the outline of the cheeks, but the top extends to take in the shackle hole (FIG. 12-3C). The holes in the cheeks are to fit the 3/8-inch reduced screwed ends of the spacers and the axle, but the central piece has to fit over the 1/2-inch diameter rods.

Make the axle (FIG. 12-3D) of sufficient length between the shoulders to take the central piece and the two sheaves with working clearance. Drill lubrication holes similar to those in the single block.

Make the two spacers (FIG. 12-3E) the same size as the axle. Make two collars (FIG. 12-3F) to hold the divider central. At the axle, it merely slides over, without any distance pieces.

After a trial assembly, tighten all nuts and lightly rivet over them. Shackle screws should also be locked by riveting or wiring. Ropes are best taken around metal thimbles, to reduce wear, and should either be securely knotted or spliced to the thimbles or shackles.

13

Rod and Bar Bender

It is unwise to try to bend most metals sharply. They will keep a better shape, with no risk of cracking, if they are bent to moderate curves. Without some sort of jig to control movement, it is difficult to make a neat even bend. This tool (FIG. 13-1) is intended to bend rods up to 5/8-inch diameter and flat strips up to 1/2-inch-by-1 1/4-inch section. Different thicknesses bend best at different curves. For round rods, an internal radius of the bend equal to twice the diameter of the rod is satisfactory, so 3/8-inch rod bends around a 1 1/2-inch diameter die, 1/2-inch rod bends around a 2-inch diameter die, and 5/8-inch rod bends around a 2 1/2-inch diameter die.

The tool has a base plate with a block for the metal being bent to press against. On this is mounted an arm, which carries the internal die, and a roller, which forces the rod or bar around it, using an extension tube as a lever. All of the parts may be mild steel, but if considerable use is expected the bolts should be high tensile steel. The dies and roller may also be a harder steel.

Make the base from 1/2-inch plate (FIG. 13-2A). It is shown with three feet (FIG. 13-2B), which give clearance for bolt heads below and allows you to fix screws to a bench. The feet are round and could be welded to the base. Three feet will stand firm if the surface below is uneven, where four feet might not; this may be an advantage if the bender is to be used away from the shop.

The block (FIG. 13-2C) has to resist the bending thrust and should be secured with 1/2-inch bolts. The bending arm has to be moved to different positions to suit internal dies for different diameters of rod or thicknesses of bar. The first position suits 3/8-inch or less, and the others are for 1/2-inch or 5/8-inch. Mark the position of the first hole (FIG. 13-2D) and draw a line at 30° to its line for the positions of the other holes (FIG. 13-2E).

These and all the other holes through the base may be for 1/2-inch bolts. Bolts with full heads and nuts can be used, except the two cor-

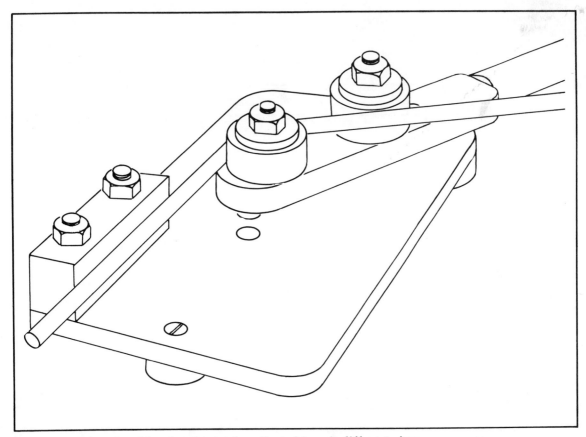

FIG. 13-1. This rod and bar bender can be adjusted to suit different sizes.

ner holes through the feet (FIG. 13-2F), which take countersunk heads, so the bending arm will pass over.

The bending arm (FIG. 13-3A) is 3/4-inch-by-1 1/2-inch section. The pivot for the internal die passes through a 3/4-inch hole (FIG. 13-3B). There are two positions for the 1/2-inch bolt holding the bending roller (FIG. 13-3C). The end extends far enough to come under the largest internal die. Reduce the other end to 3/4-inch diameter, so a piece of tube about 36 inches long can be slipped over to provide leverage. If you alter sizes, make sure the reduced part of the arm will clear the corners of the base when it is pulled around, so the tube does not catch on them. The arm could be made longer, in any case, if you wish. Soft or thin metals can then be bent without adding the tube.

Make the pivot for the internal die (FIG. 13-3E) with a bore to take a 1/2-inch bolt. The part to fit the die is 1 inch high and 1 inch in diameter. Reduce to make a hand push fit in the hole in the arm, with enough clearance to allow movement and provide a top to retain the die.

Make the dies as collars to fit over the pivot (FIG. 13-3F). There are three: 1 1/2-inch, 2-inch and 2 1/2-inch diameter. Although a die does not have to revolve on the pivot, it should be loose enough on the neck of the pivot and under the top to allow it to respond to the metal being pulled around it.

The pivot for the bending roller (FIG. 13-3G) does not go through the arm, but is otherwise similar to the other pivot. The roller (FIG. 13-3H) is the same as the smallest internal die. It has

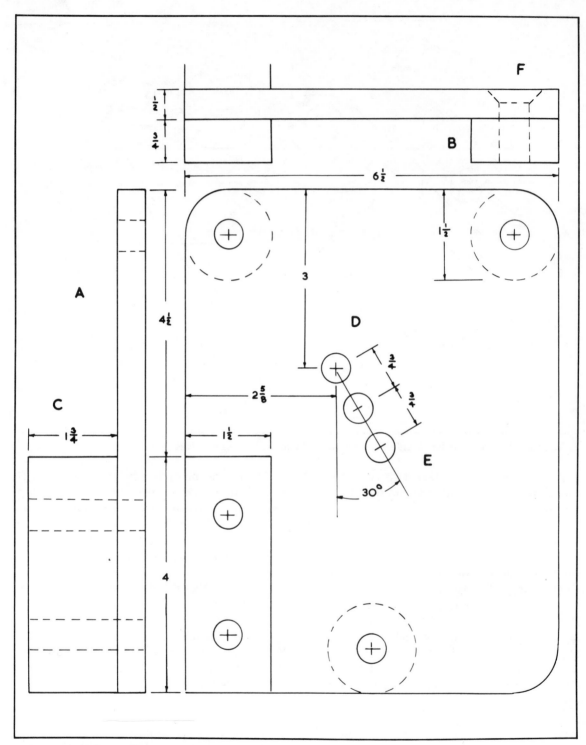

FIG. 13-2. Sizes and layout of the main parts of the rod bender.

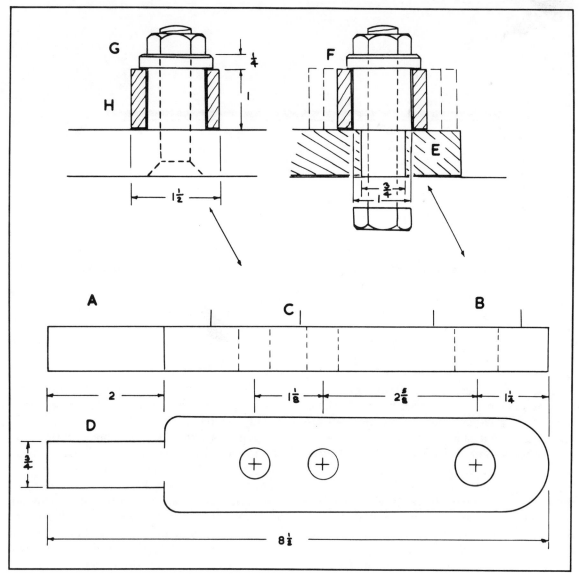

FIG. 13-3. The bending arm (A-D) and dies (E-H).

to revolve as it is pulled around, so give it a working clearance. Make sure the countersunk screw head is below the surface.

Graphite lubrication of the moving parts may be better than grease. Test the action on various diameters and thicknesses with the dies and rollers at different positions.

14

Gimbals

A vessel of any size at sea rolls and pitches to varying degrees, with smaller craft experiencing the most violent motion. Sailing craft are steadied by their sails, but they often cruise for long periods some way off vertical. In all these conditions, the magnetic compass used for steering and navigation has to remain level if it is to give accurate readings. Traditionally, the compass is arranged to swing in all directions necessary to remain level with an arrangement of rings, called *gimbals* (FIG. 14-1). The case it is mounted in may be cylindrical metal or a wooden box.

There are other uses for gimbals on a yacht. Oil lamps are used for decoration and to conserve electricity. If they are not kept level they will smoke. A single burner cooker, used to heat meals when under way, has to be kept level to function properly and to avoid spillage from a pan on it.

Gimbals for a compass must be nonmagnetic metal so the needle is not deflected. It may be possible to use nonmagnetic stainless steel,

but it is more usual to use bronze or gun metal. Brass is possible, but in a salt-laden atmosphere it will corrode.

In gimbals, the rings carry pivots at right angles to each other. In some cases, it may be possible to attach to the round casing of the compass or lamp and dispense with the inner ring, but it is usually better to have a ring so the compass or other contents can be lifted out. The compass, lamp, or cooker must have weight far enough below the level of the pivots to give a pendulum action to maintain level when the container tilts. Some compasses are weighted for this reason. When there is ample weight low enough, the gimbal rings can be arranged at the same level. If there is not enough inherent low weight, the inner ring can be slung below the other. How much depends on circumstances. A compass or lamp may be dropped about 1 inch. To keep a cooker with a pan of water on it steady may mean dropping several inches.

Sizes depend on the compass or other article. As drawn (FIG. 14-2), it is assumed the com-

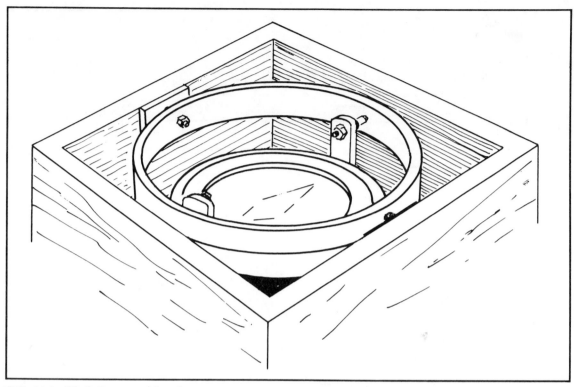

FIG. 14-1. Gimbals are used to keep a compass level despite movements of a boat.

pass case is 5 inches diameter, and the gimbals fit inside a wooden box 8 inches square inside. The parts are all made from strip, 3/16-inch-by 1/2-inch, and all the screws are 3/16-inch diameter. The inner ring is shown dropped 1 inch, but it could be level or dropped more, as required.

Make the inner ring to fit the compass case (FIG. 14-2A), so the rim rests over the metal. Make the outer ring (FIG. 14-2B) so there is a gap of 1/2 inch between the two rings. In this case, the inside of the inner ring is 5 inches diameter, and with the rings 3/16-inch thick, the inside of the outer ring is 6 3/8-inch diameter. Mark the positions of the pivots on the rings. Exact squareness between these points is important for accurate leveling, because the box angle changes with movement of the vessel.

Make the uprights (FIG. 14-2C) to the length required if the inner ring is to be lowered. Tap the ring so these can be screwed on (FIG. 14-2D).

The pivots are pointed bearings, with screw ends at 60° fitting matching hollows. After the screws are adjusted, they are locked with nuts, preferably on both sides.

For the pivots between the rings (FIG. 14-2E), make pieces of screwed rod 1 inch long. Put a screwdriver slot at one end and a 60° point at the other. Tap holes in the tops of the uprights to match (FIG. 14-2F). Make matching hollows to take the points about halfway through the outer ring.

The pivots for the outer ring (FIG. 14-2G) are made of similar screwed rods through holes tapped in the ring (FIG. 14-2H). For attaching to the box, make two plates (FIG. 14-2J), with screw holes and hollows to match the pivot screws (FIG. 14-2K).

Assemble and adjust the gimbals from the compass outwards, locking the pivot screws when the action is satisfactory. Graphite may be used on the bearings.

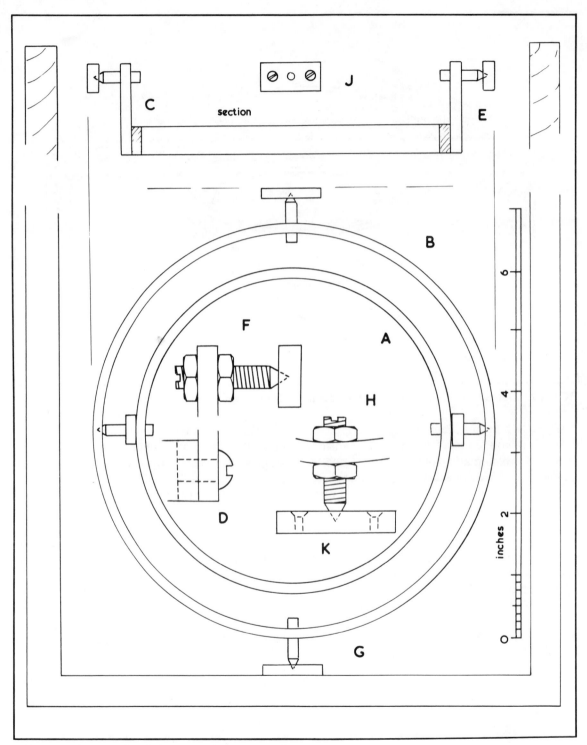

FIG. 14-2. Constructional details of the rings and pivots that form gimbals.

15

Multiple Paper Punch

Most paper punches intended for desk use will only make one or a pair of holes in one or a few sheets of paper. They are of fragile construction and only intended for occasional use.

Ring binders and other paper filing systems do not all have the same hole spacing. If your binders are imported as well as home produced, there could be a variety of spacings and any number of holes from two to six. It is possible to buy paper with holes correctly spaced, but those leaves may not always be available, and then there are other drawings, photographs, and individual entries that you may wish to include in the binder.

This multiple paper punch (FIG. 15-1) is robust and is more of a shop tool, intended to punch whatever arrangement you wish in anything up to ten or more sheets at the same time. The punches can be moved to guide holes to suit the particular pattern needed, and there are stops to locate the paper in the set position each time. The holes punched are 3/16-inch diameter, which should suit most binders and filing sys-

tems. Operation is with a lever pressed by hand, but a cord from the bar on it could be taken to a foot stirrup, leaving both hands free to manipulate the paper.

The punches should be made of tool steel. The springs on them should be spring steel. In both cases, they should be hardened and tempered. The die plate may also be tool steel, but it should have a reasonable life if made of mild steel. The other parts may be mild steel. The tool is shown mounted on a wood base. The waste pieces of paper drop through and will have to be cleared occasionally. If much punching is anticipated, it would be better to make the base the lid of a shallow box, which will collect the paper punchings.

Details are given of the end of the paper punch (FIG. 15-2A). Its length will depend on the maximum spacing of holes required. This could be up to 9 inches, which means a tool nearly 12 inches long. Any reasonable number and spacing of holes is possible. Check the files and binders you expect to have to fit and space

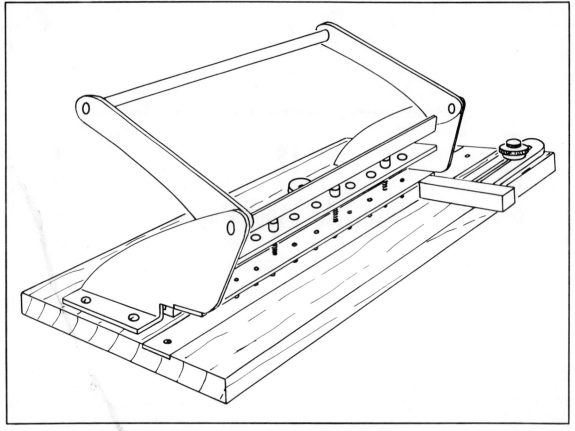

FIG. 15-1. A paper punch for making holes at selected spacings.

punch positions to suit. Of course, holes in one system may be found to form part of another system, so you can economize in the number of punch holes. For strength reasons, it would be unwise to put holes too close together. Unless the hole arrangements have to be less, try to make 3/4-inch the minimum between hole centers.

Make the pair of ends (FIGS. 15-2B, 15-3A) from 1/8-inch plate. The feet bend outwards to take wood screws into the base and leave a gap of 5/16 inch under the bottom punch guide. Mark the position of the upper guide. The pivot hole is for a 3/16-inch or 1/4-inch rivet.

Make the levers from 1/8-inch plate (FIG. 15-2C, 15-3B). Drill for the pivot and 1/4 inch for the bar. Mark the position of the pressure bar. As the lever is pressed down, this bar will slide

across the tops of the punches, so arrange it near one edge of the punch top in the up position (FIG. 15-2D). A temporary assembly will show the action and amount of movement needed.

The die plate (FIG. 15-3C) and the punch guide strips (FIG. 15-3D, E) have to be made and assembled with their holes exactly in line. Mark out the hole positions together. All are 1/8-inch thick. The lower guide strip (FIG. 15-3E) is 3/4-inch wide (FIG. 15-3F) to make the ends of the punches more easily seen, but the others are 1-inch wide.

The die plate should be made long enough to reach the ends of the base, then the groove in the wood can be cut from edge to edge. Holes in the top guide strip are 3/8-inch diameter (FIG. 15-3G). The others are 3/16. Put wood screw

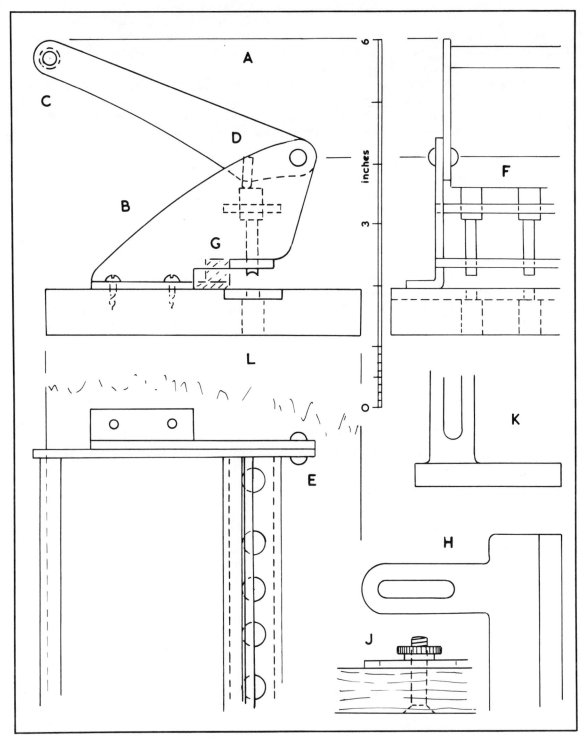

FIG. 15-2. General arrangement of the multiple paper punch.

holes at the ends of the base.

Brazing is suggested for joining the punch guides to the ends and the pressure bar to the levers. Strength is improved with tenons. Fit the top punch guide (FIG. 15-3H) with tenons into the ends (FIG. 15-3J). Make the tenon a loose fit so the silver solder can flow through. Fit the bottom guide into the recesses in the sides (FIG. 15-3K).

The pressure bar is 1/8-inch-by-1/2-inch strip. Round the lower edge, which will press on the punches. Make the lever bar (FIG. 15-3L) from 3/8-inch round rod. Make the lengths of these parts to hold the levers at a suitable spacing to fit between the sides. Use tenons on the pressure bar (FIG. 15-3M) and shoulder the ends of the lever bar. Braze these joints. If the tenons of the pressure bar or excess solder extend, level it, so the lever moves inside the ends. Mount the lever assembly with rivets (FIG. 15-2E) or nuts and bolts.

The number of punches you make will depend on how many holes you wish to punch at one time. A few spares will take care of any unexpected needs. They are made from 3/8-inch diameter tool steel rod, shouldered to 3/16-inch diameter (FIG. 15-3N). A spring encircles the punch for a length of 5/8 inch. It may be necessary to adjust the length of the reduced end of the punch to allow for slight variations in a particular machine, so make the end a little too long to allow for fitting.

Make coil springs (FIG. 15-3P) of a size that will slide on the small diameter of the punch, but will pass through a 3/8-inch hole. The uncompressed length of the spring should be 5/8 inch, but when pressure is put on it, should compress to at least 3/8 inch.

When a punch is in position, its top should project 5/16 inch above the top guide strip (FIG. 15-2F). The cutting end should then be about 3/16 inch above the die plate. When a punch is pressed down to its limit, the cutting end of the punch should go halfway through the hole in the die plate. Sharpen each punch by making an almost semicircular hollow across its end.

Harden and temper the end. Check that the punches and springs can be put into any position and will penetrate sufficiently to cut through paper.

A back stop is needed to regulate the distance paper is pushed into the tool. It is unlikely that holes will be needed closer than 3/8 inch or more than 1 inch from an edge. The back stop suggested comes up to the edge of the bottom punch guide (FIG. 15-2G). If it is needed closer, make it to pass under the guide.

Make the back stop from 1/8-inch plate of a length to slide between the tool ends and with two extensions for screwing down (FIG. 15-2H). At the edge that will come against the paper, add a strip 3/8-inch square. This could be brazed on or held with a few screws from below. The extensions have slots so a 1/4-inch screw projecting from the wood base can have 1 inch of movement and lock the stop at any position with a knurled wing, or butterfly nut (FIG. 15-2J).

One edge of the paper can be controlled with an end stop (FIG. 15-2K). This is made from 1/8-inch plate with a 3/8-inch square strip along its edge. How long the slotted extension is depends on how far the edge of the paper has to be for a particular hole configuration. If the paper needs to go far outside the metal parts of the punch, the wooden base will have to be long at that side. It may be possible to scheme holes in the guides for paper with a long extension, towards the other end of the tool, so the end stop can be kept short. For smaller papers the edge of the end stop slides along the bottom punch guide.

The base may be 3/4-inch wood. Groove it to take the die plate, and drill 3/8-inch holes to clear the paper punchings (FIG. 15-2L). Where the screws for the stops come, it helps to tap the wood so the threads grip. If necessary, the countersunk screws may be secured with epoxy adhesive. The wood base may be varnished and most of the metal parts protected with paint.

If foot operation is to be used, fasten down the base, or preferably, the box which collects paper punchings. Attach a cord to the center of

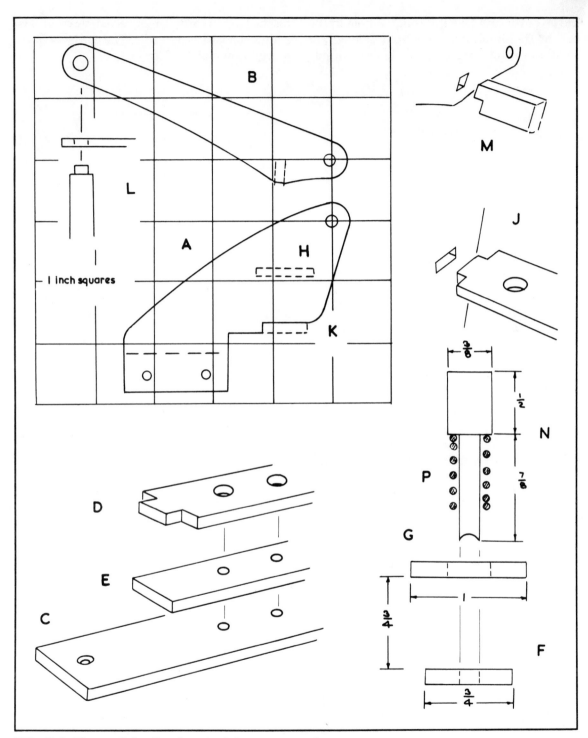

FIG. 15-3. Sizes and details of parts of the paper punch.

the lever bar and take it through a hole in the bench. The simplest foot control is a length of wood to go under the foot, with holes each side for the looped cord. A more sensitive control is a hinged board as a treadle. The cord will have to pull down about 2 inches.

16
Jib Furling Gear

The forward triangular sail of a yacht, called the *jib*, has to be controlled from the cockpit aft. It is often difficult and sometimes dangerous to get at it by going forward when it is necessary to lower or replace the sail with a smaller one when conditions get too rough for its use. If the sail can be rolled up completely or partially without going onto the foredeck, bad weather conditions can be taken care of conveniently and safely. This may be done by use of the *Wykeham Martin furling gear*, named after the man who devised it a long time ago.

At the tack of the sail (FIG. 16-1A) there is a spool, which can be pulled around by a rope, which is led aft. At the top, a swivel allows the sail to rotate as the spool at the bottom is turned (FIG. 16-1B). The sail should have a wire *luff rope*; then when the rope on the spool uncoils, the sail winds around the luff rope (FIG. 16-1C), either completely or partially. The action is reversed and the sail unwound by pulling on

the sheets, which control the sail in use (FIG. 16-1D).

This furling gear has a spool enclosing a ball bearing. There is a guide for the controlling rope. A ring is shown for attaching to the stem fitting of the boat and a pin through jaws to attach to the eye in the sail (FIG. 16-1E). The arrangement can be modified to suit the attachment points on boat and sail. The top swivel (FIG. 16-1F) has a similar bearing, and is shown with an eye and jaws, which may be altered.

The sizes given should suit a small yacht up to 25 feet long, but they could be increased for larger sails or reduced slightly for a smaller sailing boat.

The most suitable metal is bronze, which has a good resistance to salt water. Brass could be used on inland waters. Steel would have to be well protected by galvanizing or paint. The steel ball races are enclosed and packed with

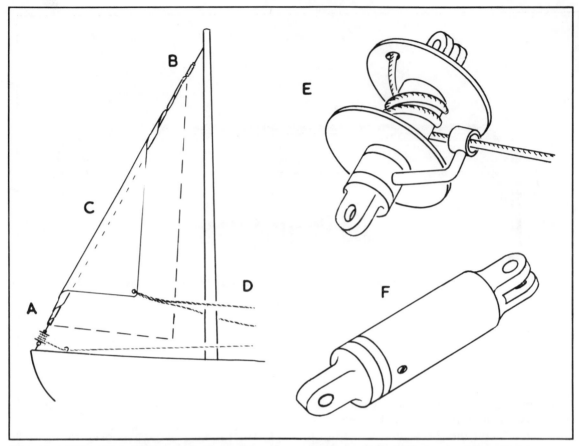

FIG. 16-1. With jib furling gear the foresail can be wound around its luff rope to reduce its area.

grease, so they should not rust. The grub screws, which hold the parts together, are best made of stainless steel.

Tack Spool

The *spool swivel* (FIG. 16-2) has a reel with the top to take the pin included (FIG. 16-2A). The lower ring is the head of a screw (FIG. 16-2B), which forms the pivot for the rope guide (FIG. 16-2C) and the internal assembly.

The spool could be turned from solid metal or the two flanges made from sheet metal brazed to a solid rod (FIG. 16-2D). At the top, cut down to make a gap to take the sail eye and thin the outside to two flanges (FIG. 16-2E). Mark the centers of the holes and round the ends. Bore inside to take the revolving parts. Check the size

of a suitable ball bearing and adjust to suit. The suggested size should suit a 1-inch bearing (FIG. 16-2F).

Turn the screw (FIG. 16-2G) with a 7/16-inch diameter stem and a shoulder of 1-inch diameter. Reduce the end to 3/8 inch (FIG. 16-2H) or to suit the stem fitting on the boat. Round the end and drill a 3/8-inch hole. Turn the plug to be a push fit in the spool (FIG. 16-2J), with a 7/16-inch hole to suit the pivot screw.

The rope guide (FIG. 16-2C, K) may be built up. Turn a collar to slide over the pivot screw. Tap a hole in its side for a piece of 1/4-inch rod. Bend the rod, and shoulder its other end so it can be fitted into a short piece of tube. Well round the inside and outside of the tube, so the rope will not chafe. Braze both ends of the rod.

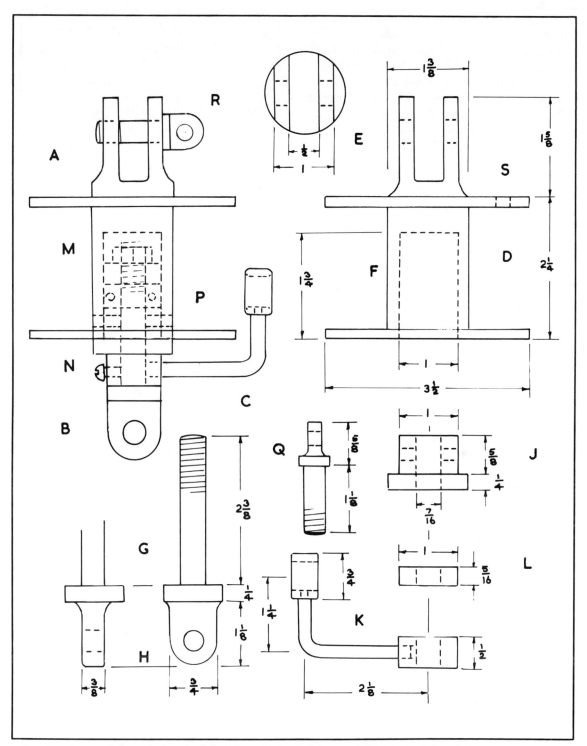

FIG. 16-2. Parts of the spool swivel forming the bottom part of the jib furling gear.

Make the internal collar (FIG. 16-2L) to fit above the ball bearing. This could be steel or gun metal. Tap a hole through its center to fit the pivot screw. Cut a thread on the screw long enough to go through the collar and take a locknut (FIG. 16-2M). Test the assembly with the rope guide and plug. The rope guide does not have to pivot freely, but when the furling gear is mounted on the boat, it should be possible to turn the guide to give the best lead to the rope, and it may not have to be moved again. A set screw may be used to lock the guide when the best position has been found (FIG. 16-2N). Of course, the collar should hold the ball race only sufficiently tightly for the easiest possible rotation.

Drill the spool and the plug to take two 3/16-inch grub screws (FIG. 16-2P). The hole can go right through the plug, for ease in cutting threads, but the screws should drive flush with the spool surface and not reach the pivot screw on which the plug rotates.

Make a trial assembly dry. If this is satisfactory, make sure the locknut is securing the collar, then pack inside with grease and assemble the parts.

Make the pin for the top (FIG. 16-2A) from 1/2-inch rod, turned down to 3/8-inch diameter (FIG. 16-2Q), with the top thinned to 1/4 inch and rounded and drilled (FIG. 16-2R), for tightening with pliers and locking with wire. The pin passes through one side and screws into the

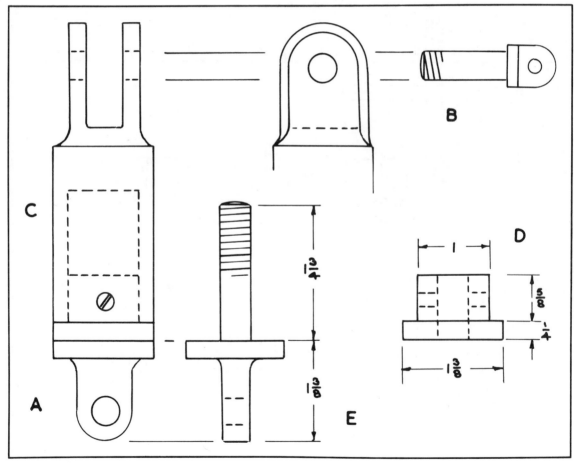

FIG. 16-3. Details of the top swivel of the jib furling gear.

other. Alternatively, drill clearance holes on both sides and use a nut and bolt.

Drill a hole in the top flange to take the end of the rope (FIG. 16-2S). A suitable rope for a small yacht would be 5/16-inch diameter, but make the hole larger and round its edges. In use, the rope around the drum has its end knotted outside.

Top Swivel

The top swivel (FIG. 16-3) has a similar action to the spool but is without the flanges and the rope guide. Make it in the same way with similar materials. It is shown with an eye at one end (FIG. 16-3A) and a pin at the other (FIG. 16-3B). It can be used either way up or there could be pins

or eyes at both ends.

Make the case (FIG. 16-3C) similar to the hub of the spool, with provision for a pin or an eye at the end. Make a plug (FIG. 16-3D) similar to that of the spool. Drill the case and the plug for two screws, which could be grub screws similar to those on the spool, although it would not matter if the heads projected on this part.

Make the screw (FIG. 16-3E) similar to that of the spool, but shorter, as it does not have to pass through a rope guide. Make the internal collar and thread these parts to hold the ball race.

If the parts function correctly during a trial dry assembly, pack with grease and the two swivels will be ready for use.

17

Adjustable Lamp

Being able to get a light directed exactly where you want it is valuable in several activities. In the shop, there may be precision marking or machining where you could make a mistake in poor light. A drawing board should have a movable light. For sewing and other needle crafts, a light directed at fine work is of more use than general lighting. Primarily, such a lamp has to be functional. It could be made ornate, but fitness for purpose is probably the main contribution to good looks.

This adjustable lamp (FIG. 17-1) has hinged parallel arms. They are shown 12 inches long, which should give a good spread, but they could be made of other lengths, and the two pairs do not have to match. They swing between plates with fiber or rubber washers providing friction to keep the arms at any setting. The base adds weight, and it can be screwed down to a desk or work top or be given a broad wooden bottom, so the lamp can be moved about. At the other end, there is a universal fitting to attach to a lamp unit, which can be tilted in any direction.

The whole assembly may be made of steel. For shop use, it might be left untreated, but for most purposes it would be better if painted, preferably the individual parts before assembly. If the nuts, bolts, and washers are plated, they would enhance appearance. The pivot plates may be a different color to the arms. The whole unit may be made of brass and polished for an attractive effect on a desk or sewing table.

The arms are 3/8-inch-by-1/2-inch section, and the plates are 1/8-inch thick. The base swivel parts are turned from solid blocks.

The arms pivot between pairs of plates. If the pivot bolts are arranged as described, the arms will move from almost flat together, for storage, or extend outwards or upwards almost to the combined length of the arms. Downward movement is not as great.

Make the pairs of plates first. The pivot between the arms has pairs of holes at 60° (FIG. 17-2A). Mark out by drawing two lines at 60° and position the holes on them (FIG. 17-3A). With

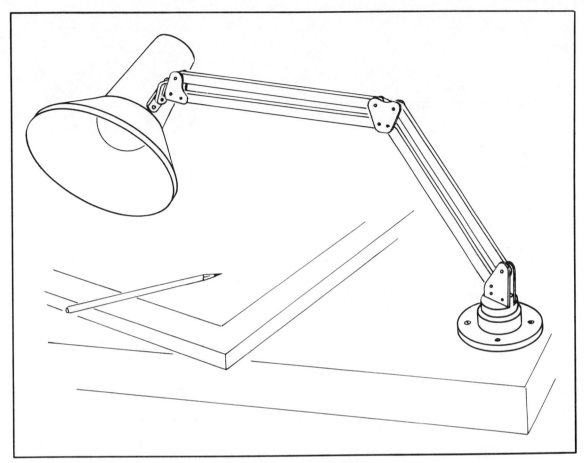

FIG. 17-1. This adjustable lamp can be moved to many positions.

the holes as centers, draw 3/8-inch radius corners and join them. The outline could be straight, but a hollow on the long edge improves appearance.

The plates at the lamp unit (FIG. 17-2B) are marked out by first locating two holes on a line; the other hole is off center in relation to them (FIG. 17-3B). Mark the outline in a similar way to the first pair of plates.

The plates at the base (FIG. 17-2C) have the arm holes 1 1/2 inches apart on a line 45° to the bottom edge (FIG. 17-4A). Draw the line and holes, then find the center between them and drop a vertical line down. Make the bottom edge symmetrical about this. Mark two holes for bolts through the base pivot.

All parts are assembled with nuts and bolts. Their diameter is not critical—3/16 inch is suitable—but slightly different sized bolts or screws may be used. The heads may be for a wrench or screwdriver. For quick adjustment of friction, one nut at each pair of plates may be a knurled- or butterfly-type. Drill the plates to suit the chosen bolts. Round or take off sharpness of the plate edges.

For the universal joint at the lamp end of the assembly, make a T-section block to fit between the plates and a pad to screw onto the lamp unit (FIG. 17-3C). Make the leg of the block the same thickness as the arm (FIG. 17-3D). Its other part extends downwards to take a nut and bolt (FIG. 17-3E). Make sure there is sufficient

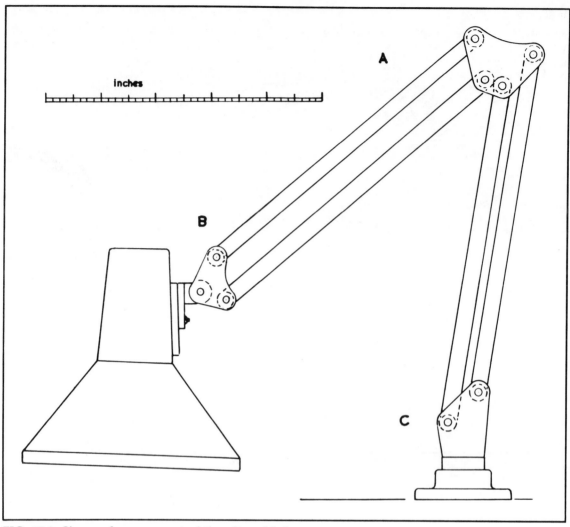

inches

A

B

C

FIG. 17-2. Sizes and arrangement of the adjustable lamp.

clearance under the leg part for a washer and nut. Round all corners. Keep the face of the block flat. The pad (FIG. 17-3F) is a flat piece with rounded ends to take a countersunk screw through the block and two screws into the lamp unit. Its size and shape may have to be modified to suit a particular lamp and shade unit.

At the base of the plates fit each side of a lug on a turned part (FIG. 17-4B), which fits into the base (FIG. 17-4C). This part is made from 1 1/2-inch round rod, with its end reduced to 3/4-inch (FIG. 17-4D). Cut the lug the same thick-

ness as the arms and drill it for bolts.

The thickness of the base should be slightly more than the length of the part that fits into it so that does not project through (FIG. 17-4E). Round the exposed edges. Bore so the arm assembly will pivot smoothly, but be tight enough to stay in any set position. Drill for screws. If there is to be a separate wood base it could be round, square, or octagonal. If made from 1-inch wood and about 9 inches across, it will give stability with a moderate reach.

The arms (FIG. 17-4F) are all the same. Drill

for screws and round the ends.

It may be possible to get sufficient friction in a metal-to-metal assembly, but it is easier to make the parts stay where you put them, particularly if the lamp unit is heavy, if you put in friction washers. These may be fiber or rubber. It would be possible to cut suitable ones from leather. In some joints, there could be metal washers, but it will be best to use friction washers in every place. Use metal washers under the bolt heads and nuts (FIG. 17-4G). You could use stiff nuts so they lock on the screws, but there should be very little tendency for nuts to work loose, and it should be satisfactory to have plain nuts (FIG. 17-4H). Choose bolts that project only slightly through the nuts. Allow for a knurled or wing nut at one place on each plate, if you wish.

The electric cable can be led around the outer arms, with some slack over the joints. Make a few clips (FIG. 17-4J) to hold the cable to the arms. Strip copper, 1/4-inch wide and 1/16-inch or less thick, can be used.

Make a trial assembly, then separate the parts for painting.

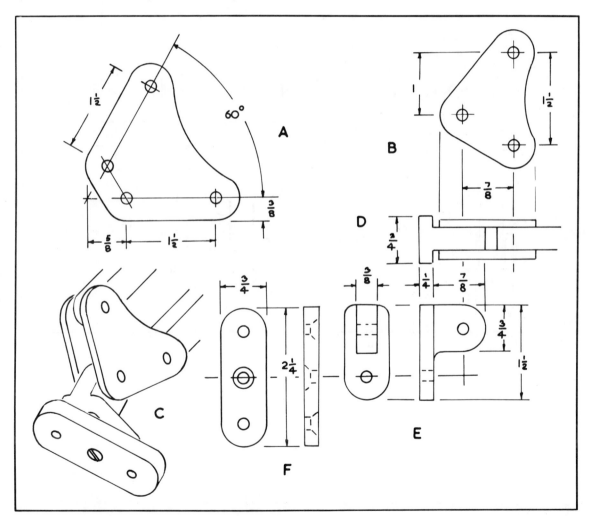

FIG. 17-3. Hinge parts of the adjustable lamp.

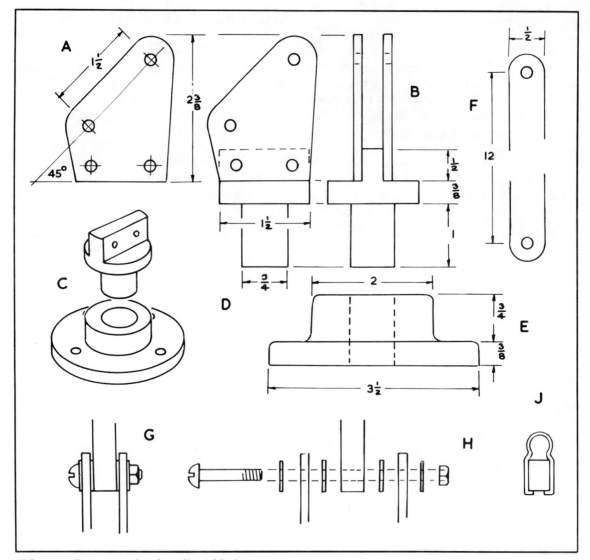

FIG. 17-4. Base parts for the adjustable lamp.

18

Photographic Pan and Tilt Head

The simplest tripod for a camera has a screw to fit the camera and hold it level. That is not always what is wanted. It is more convenient to be able to move the camera about and lock it at the position you want. This means incorporating a universal movement, so the camera can swing from side to side as well as tilt to any reasonable angle. This applies to still and movie cameras. If the camera has to swing around to follow action, it is said to *pan*.

This head (FIG. 18-1A) is intended to fit onto the tripod screw. On the base that takes the screw (FIG. 18-1B), there is a horizontal pivot (FIG. 18-1C), which can be locked at any position with a screw having a lever handle (FIG. 18-1D).

Attached to this is the tilt head (FIG. 18-1E) on a pivot screw, to which it can be locked by turning a long handle (FIG. 18-1F). The handle allows you to direct the camera as you wish, then a turn of it locks the tilt action.

On the tilt head is a strip of metal, with a screw and locknut for attaching the camera (FIG. 18-1G). The strip could be short, if that is all you need, but two other functions are shown. If you want to mount the camera so it faces downwards for a picture of something on the ground, or to take a picture with an upright format, there is another position square to the first (FIG. 18-1H). Most cameras will take a flash unit on top in a shoe, but for many subjects, it is better to have lighting coming from one side. An extension (FIG. 18-1J) allows the flash unit to be mounted there and joined to the camera with a cable.

The sizes suggested will suit most 35mm cameras, but it may be advisable to check your camera size. This pan and tilt head may be made of steel, brass, or aluminum. The reason for using a stand for a camera is mainly to provide steadiness, so it is unwise to attempt to ligthen the parts much, as that might lead to vibration. If you alter sizes, keep the camera position reasonably close to the top of the tripod. The flash extension may be of almost any length.

The standard camera thread takes a 1/4-inch-by-20-t.p.i. screw. It is convenient to use the same threads for other parts on this

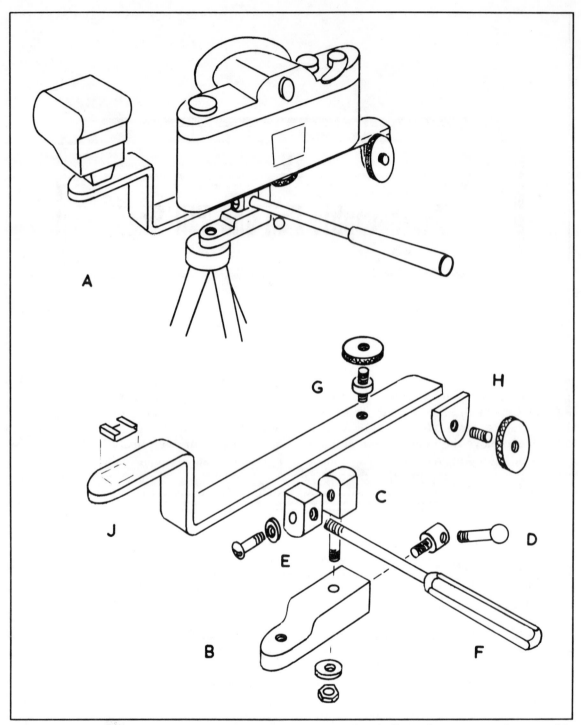

FIG. 18-1. A photographic pan and tilt head mounts on a tripod and allows the camera to be moved to and locked at many positions.

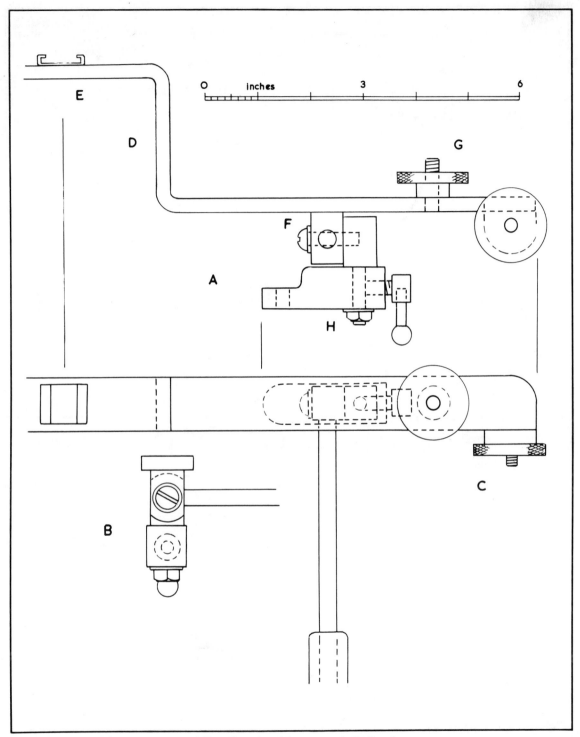

FIG. 18-2. General arrangement of the photographic pan and tilt head.

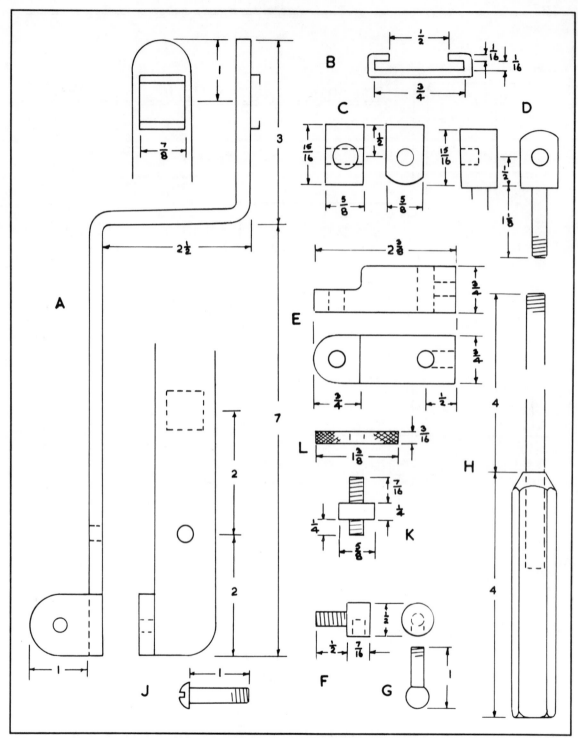

FIG. 18-3. Sizes and the parts of the photographic pan and tilt head.

head, except for the handle, which will be stiffer if a 5/16-inch diameter screw is used. Those parts which are not screwed may be brazed. They can be joined with two small countersunk screws at each place. The tilt head block may have a 1/4-inch diameter lug turned on it, to either screw to the flat strip or be taken through it and riveted. It is best to delay drilling until all parts are made and hole positions marked.

The general drawing (FIG. 18-2) shows the layout. The pivoting and turning assembly (FIG. 18-2A, B) must clear the tripod head. If the vertical camera position is to be made (FIG. 18-2C), check that the camera will be clear of the tripod legs.

The top strip (FIG. 18-2D) is made from 1/4-inch-by-1-inch strip, cranked to raise the flash unit (FIG. 18-3A). Mark the positions of holes and round the edges and ends.

Check the flash unit to get the size to make the shoe. The usual sizes are shown (FIG. 18-3B), but because the shoe must be a push fit, the two parts should be matched during construction. If you will want to use the flash unit either way, the shoe must be parallel, but for one-way use there could be a slight taper so the unit tightens as it is pushed in. When you have a satisfactory fit, mount the shoe in position (FIG. 18-3E).

The two tilt parts are 5/8-inch square section. They are cut to have clearance at the ends, which are curved. Make the upper part (FIG. 18-3C) to braze to the strip or with a lug to screw or rivet on. Make the lower part (FIG. 18-3D) with a 1/4-inch diameter extension, which forms the *panning pivot*.

The panning pivot goes through the base (FIG. 18-3E). Make it 3/4-inch square section. Reduce the end that will go on the tripod top to 3/8-inch thick and mark its hole. The pivot hole goes through. Mark the end of the block for the locking screw.

The locking screw is given a lever with a knob on its end, so it is easily found by touch when your eyes are concerned with sighting the camera. Make the screw with a cylindrical head (FIG. 18-3F). Turn the lever (FIG. 18-3G) and screw it into the side of the head.

Make the lever (FIG. 18-3H) about 8 inches long, to give control when you are looking through the camera viewfinder. This is 5/16-inch diameter rod, threaded on the end. Give it a wood or plastic grip. For ease of turning the handle, make the grip octagonal. It can be joined to the metal rod with epoxy glue.

Join the two pivot parts (FIG. 18-3C, D) with a 1/4-inch screw (FIG. 18-3J). The amount of thread on this and the part it fits should be adjusted so they pull tight when you have the friction needed, otherwise there is a risk of the screw loosening. Arrange a fiber washer under the screw head (FIG. 18-2F). Drill and tap the pivot piece (FIG. 18-3D) for the screw. Drill a clearance hole for the screw in the other piece (FIG. 18-3C) and another tapped hole square to it for the handle, which should tighten against the screw.

The camera could fit onto a stud in the strip, but it is shown (FIG. 18-2G) on a raised fitting with a large locknut. Turn the piece (FIG. 18-3K) with a lower part to screw into the flat strip and an upper part long enough to go through the locknut into the camera. The locknut (FIG. 18-3L) is a simple disk knurled on the outside and with a hole threaded to suit the screw.

If the alternative vertical position is being provided, that may be treated in a similar way, or the locknut may go on a simple stud.

Assemble the parts and try the action. A fiber washer may be put under the nut on the panning pivot screw (FIG. 18-2H). Graphite lubricant may be needed to make the moving parts work smoothly. Dismantle and polish or paint before final assembly.

19

Parallel-action Drafting Equipment

For precision draftsmanship, there are advanced and complex drafting machines capable of working to very fine limits, but there are many times, as when only occasional drawings are needed or when working away from an office, when something simpler would be satisfactory. An artist, a carpenter, or other craftsmen concerned with decorative or less precise work can use a drawing board with simple mechanisms. Anyone needing to draw a simple assembly to scale to show its format or details of a joint will welcome a modestly equipped drawing board.

The equipment described here provides a parallel action for a straightedge, on which triangles and other instruments can be set. It is possible to make the parts to suit any size board, but the sizes and description assume a board about 18 inches by 24 inches, with a 2 1/4-inch straightedge moving over it. The board may be 3/4-inch plywood. The straightedge should be made from a stable hardwood, 1/2-inch thick.

The straightedge is guided up and down the board with cables over pulleys at each side (FIG. 19-1). These are assemblies attached to the board and linked across it with a straightedge (FIG. 19-2A). The pulleys are mounted between parallel strips (FIG. 19-2B), with spacers at the ends.

Choose fine steel flexible cable, of the type used in some engine controls and not more than 1/16-inch diameter. This is made of several fine wires twisted together. The cable must be flexible enough to pass around 1 1/4-inch diameter wheels. The wheels and turnbuckle body may be brass, but the other parts are steel.

Make the side bars from straight steel 3/16-inch thick. The inner one (FIG. 19-3A) is 1/4 inch wider than the other (FIG. 19-3B). At the ends, make spacers from 1/2-inch square bar (FIG. 19-3C). They may be riveted or held together with 1/8-inch or 3/16-inch nuts and bolts.

For attaching to the board, there are angle brackets at about 9-inch intervals (FIG. 19-2C, 19-3D). Locate them so the top edge of the wide side bar comes level with the top of the drawing board. Screw into tapped holes in the wide

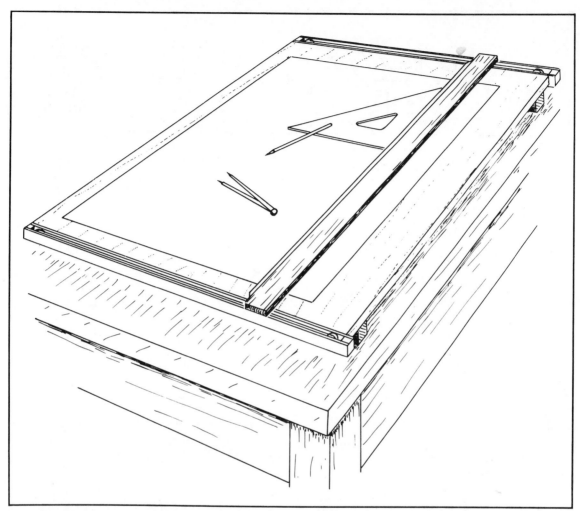

FIG. 19-1. Parallel-action drafting equipment allows a straightedge to be moved with a parallel action.

bars and drill for wood screws upwards into the board (FIG. 19-3E). Vertical slot holes in the brackets will allow for adjusting to get the metal and wood top surfaces level.

Drill through the side bars for the 1/8-inch wheel axles (FIG. 19-2D). Make the wheels (FIG. 19-3F) to fit between the side bars with enough clearance to rotate easily. Turn the grooves in the wheels deep enough to retain the cable and only wide enough to guide the cable with minimum friction.

To guide the ends of the straightedge, there are metal plates (FIG. 19-2E) let into it and blocks which are attached to the cable (FIG. 19-2F). The wood straightedge can be wider than the plate (FIG. 19-2G) and may be cut away where it comes over the ends (FIG. 19-2H). Make the 3/16-inch plate (FIG. 19-3G) with four holes for countersunk screws upwards into the straightedge. The location of the other two screws should be left until after the block has been made.

The section of the block has to be related to the spacing of the side bars and the cable over the wheels. There is a piece to move centrally between the bars (FIG. 19-2F), then a notch slides freely over the outer bar and an outer projec-

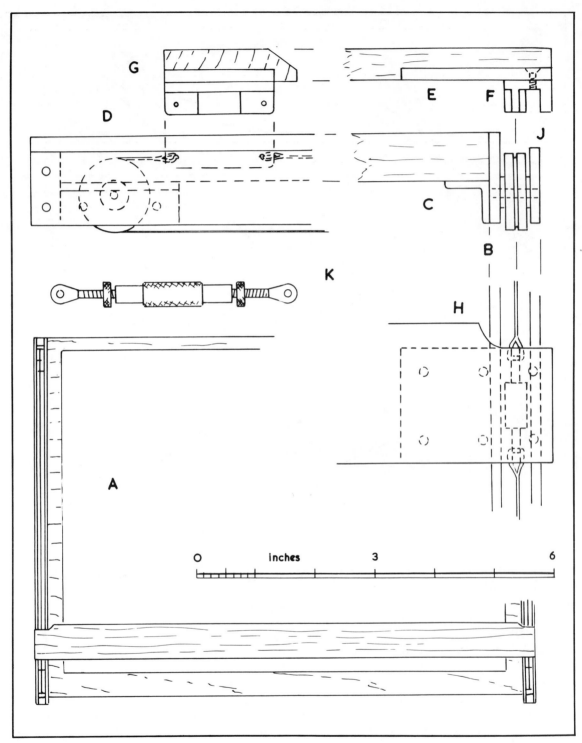

FIG. 19-2. Details of the main components of the parallel-action drafting equipment.

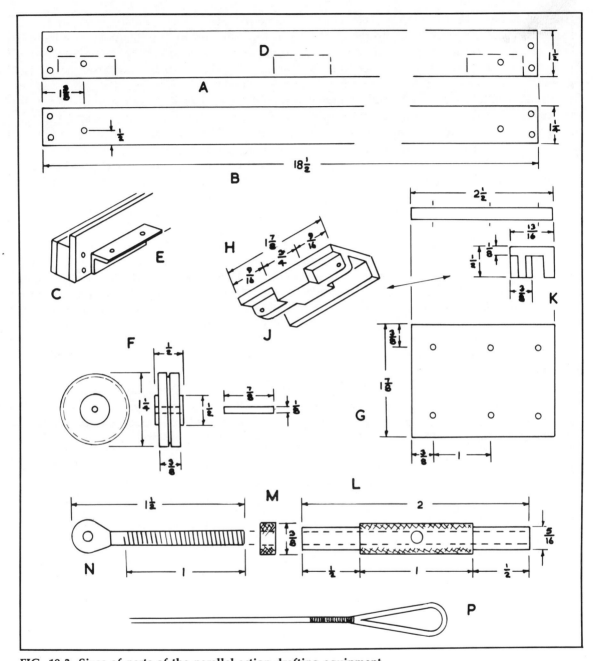

FIG. 19-3. Sizes of parts of the parallel-action drafting equipment.

tion prevents sideways movement.

The block is 1 7/8-inch long (FIG. 19-3H). Form the 3/8-inch square part with a gap beside it to slide over the outer bar. Reduce the ends of the 3/8-inch part to 1/8 inch to take loops of the cable (FIG. 19-3J). Test the free action of the blocks for the full lengths of the end assemblies. Drill the narrow parts for the cable. Round the

95

corners and edges. Drill and tap holes for countersunk screws from the plates into the blocks above the grooves (FIGS. 19-2J, 19-3K).

Tension is obtained and maintained in each cable with a turnbuckle (FIG. 19-2K) underneath. Its screws have left-handed and right-handed threads, so when the body is turned, the opposite ends can be made to move in and out, then locked with knurled nuts. A suitable size uses 1/8-inch screw threads.

Turn the turnbuckle body (FIG. 19-3L) with a tapping size hole right through and a raised knurled center. There may be a 1/8-inch hole across for a peg to be put through to aid in tightening. Make locknuts (FIG. 19-3M), also knurled and with tapping holes. The screws need eyes to take the cable (FIG. 19-3N). If the round rod is malleable, it may be possible to flatten an end and file it to shape. Otherwise, turn down from larger rod and file the ends flat. Cut left-handed and right-handed threads on opposite screws of a pair and tap the holes in the locknuts and body to match.

The ends of the cable will have to be looped through holes and locked in position. It might be possible to clamp the twisted wire under washers with small nuts and bolts, but there will be no risk of slipping if the loops are soldered. Tuck a wire end through its hole then bend it back into a long loop. Twist the wire ends around. If you can push a few through that will help. Finally, wrap around with fine copper wire (FIG. 19-3P) and solder the joint.

As you assemble, arrange the straightedge close to the bottom edge of the drawing board, then arrange the lengths of cable so the turnbuckles on the underside are close to the top edge. That will allow a full movement up and down the board.

Get the first assembly reasonably accurate. Draw a line parallel with the bottom of the drawing board about 6 inches up. Adjust the straightedge to it by working on the turnbuckles, tightening one and loosening the other until the straightedge matches the line. Practice will show how tight to tension the cables. You will have to tighten further when they have settled down after a little use. The line across the board will serve as a check whenever you make alterations.

If the board is not already raised, fit it with wood battens to lift it enough for the metal parts to be clear of the table top, or add the supports described as the next project.

20
Drawing Board Supports

A simple drawing board may be used flat on a table, but it is more convenient if it is at an angle, particularly if the user wishes to sit. An engineering draftsman may have a drafting machine, but anyone with only occasional need to make mechanical drawings has to manage with something simpler. An artist has no need for mechanical assistance, but he will be glad of a means of tilting his board. This also applies to craftwork, where a sloping board makes the work easier and more comfortable.

This tilting arrangement (FIG. 20-1) is intended for use with a board of moderate size, possibly 18 inches by 24 inches, although it may be used without alteration for boards up to 24 inches and of any reasonable length. The principle could be used with parts of other sizes, if they would suit your board. The pair of supports would suit the board with the parallel-action straightedge described as the last project.

The parts may be made of steel and painted. Brass or aluminum are also suitable. The sections specified will make a rigid assembly, al-though it will be comparatively heavy. Shakiness has to be avoided if accurate work is to be done on the board.

The main parts are 3/16-inch- or 1/4-inch-by-1-inch section. The angle brackets may be bent, but are more conveniently made from angle iron 1-inch-by-1-inch-by-1/8-inch or thicker. The rod is 3/8-inch diameter.

The arrangement shown allows for the lowest angle of board to table being 10° (FIG. 20-2A) and the steepest angle 30° (FIG. 20-2B). The board can be any standard drawing board or a piece of 3/4-inch plywood. Put a strip of 1-inch square wood (FIG. 20-2C) under the front edge, either right across or as short blocks at the corners. Round the edge the board will tilt on. This gives clearance to the supports and will lift the parallel-action strips (if fitted) clear of the table.

Mark the locations of the support parts under the board (FIG. 20-2D). It should be satisfactory to put them on lines 3 inches to 5 inches from the ends.

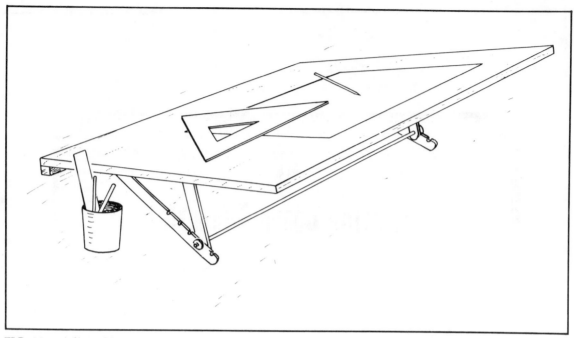

FIG. 20-1. Adjustable drawing board supports allow the board to be arranged at angles between 10° and 30° to the table.

Make the two legs (FIG. 20-3A). The ends are semicircular. Five notches are shown, but you could have more intermediate positions, if you wish. Make the notches by drilling 3/8-inch holes so they come just below the edge (FIG. 20-3B), then cut into them. Test the rod in the notches. It should fit easily, but without excessive play. Leave drilling the single holes until other parts are made.

The angle brackets (FIG. 20-3C, D) are the same. The two holes in one leg are for round-head screws into the board. The hole position the other way is shown more than halfway across so the leg end comes low enough to be clear of the board surface (FIG. 20-3E).

The two struts (FIG. 20-3F) are simple pieces with semicircular ends, but at the end that will take the rod, thicken with a circular pad (FIG. 20-3G). It could be a disk brazed or soldered on. Drill there for the rod (FIG. 20-3H).

The pivots may be rivets or bolts. Movement will only be occasional and limited, so either would be suitable and 1/4-inch diameter will do. Use locknuts on bolts.

Make the rod (FIG. 20-3J) long enough to go through slots in the legs and project a short way. It may be satisfactory to just let it drop into notches, but you can arrange to lock it in place by threading the ends. Make knurled nuts (FIGS. 20-2E, 20-3K) to fit on the ends of the rods. Solder or screw the rods into the ends of the struts.

Mark where you expect the angle brackets to come on the board, but use the length determined by the rod to get the exact spacing, so when the supports are adjusted to different angles, the legs move squarely. When you are satisfied with the assembly, take the parts off the board for painting.

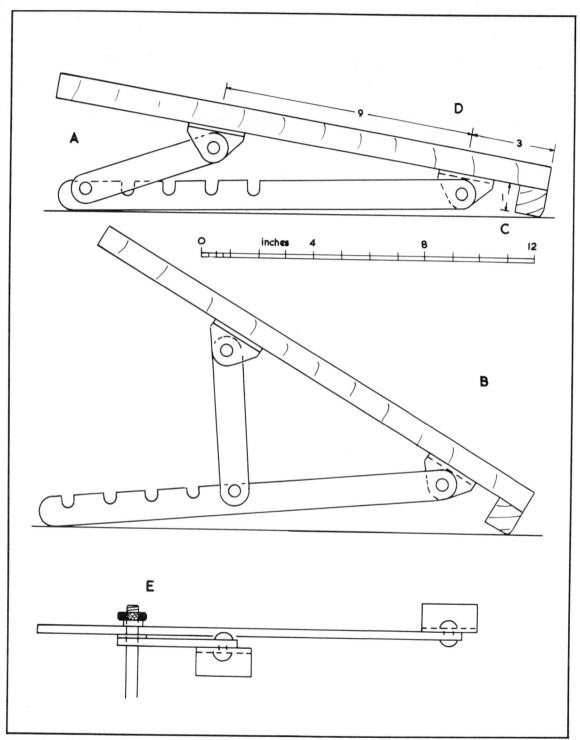

FIG. 20-2. Side views showing the equipment arranged at minimum and maximum angles.

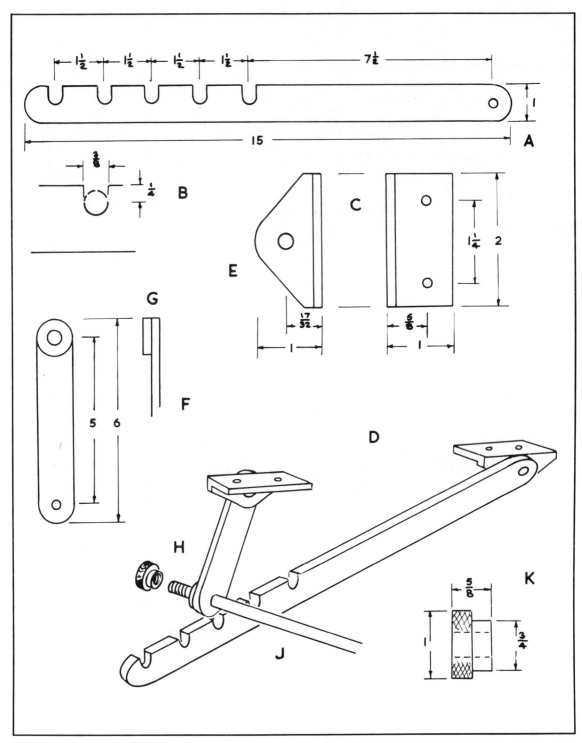

FIG. 20-3. Details of the parts of the adjustable drawing board supports.

21
Rowing Exerciser

Rowing exercises more parts of the body than may be immediately obvious. The arms pulling the oars develop a thrust down through the body to the legs. This is brought to perfection in sliding seat racing craft, where the legs bend and straighten in time with the pull of the arms, so a stroke of maximum length is achieved. In this action, leg muscles play at least as big a part as the arms in exerting as much power as possible to the oars.

By definition, in racing terms, rowing is only applied where each person pulls one oar. If one person pulls a pair of oars, he is *sculling*, and the oars are more correctly called *sculls*. However, in popular terms the action is loosely called rowing, and the word is applied in that way here.

The greatest satisfaction comes from sitting in a boat and getting our exercise using its oars, but that is not always possible, and the next best thing is a *static rowing exerciser*, used at home. This exerciser (FIG. 21-1) has a stout wooden frame with an adjustable footrest and a sliding seat. The oars or handles are on outriggers, with their ends connected to springs under the seat, so the user has to overcome this resistance as he presses his feet down, slides back on the seat, and pulls back on the grips of the oars.

Although there is more wood involved than in other projects, construction is simple. The mechanical parts are mostly steel. There is no need for ball bearings or other aids to easy running, as overcoming friction is part of the exercise. Plain bearings should run smoothly and perform adequately with light lubrication.

The dimensions given should suit a person of average size. Alternative footrest positions will adjust to most leg lengths. You may wish to experiment with other sizes to fit a particular user. Overall, the exerciser is about 54 inches by 48 inches wide and 12 inches deep. It could stand on end against a wall when out of use.

Framework

Use planed 2-inch-by-4-inch wood. The two sides are held 12 inches apart by three crosswise

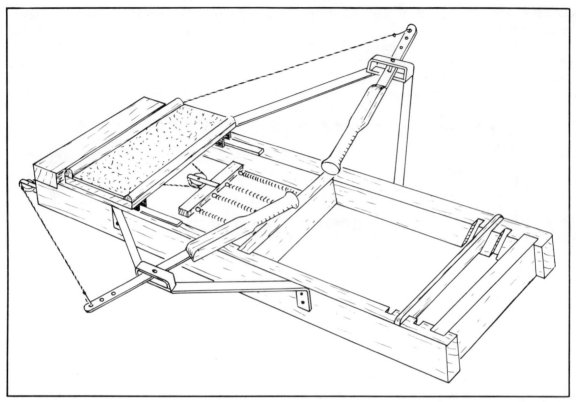

FIG. 21-1. A rowing exerciser allows the user to go through all the actions of rowing a boat.

pieces (FIG. 21-2). Mark out the two sides (FIG. 21-3A). At the feet end and midway, the crosswise pieces are notched in 3/4 inch (FIG. 21-3B) and may be screwed from outside. At the seat end, the crosswise piece is notched into the top (FIG. 21-3C) and screwed downwards. Check squareness by comparing diagonals and see that there is no twist by testing on a flat surface.

The footrest is shown with three alternative positions (FIG. 21-3D), but more could be cut, particularly if the exerciser is to be used by children and adults. The footrest has to withstand considerable pressure. It should be without flaws and may be hardwood, even if other parts are softwood. Mark the angle on a framework side and use this as a guide when cutting the ends of the footrest (FIG. 21-3E). Make the length to fit easily into the slots. Round the top edge and corners. The bottom edge need not reach the bottoms of the slots.

In a boat and on this exerciser, the feet have to be retained on the return stroke. Use a length of leather or canvas strap to make two loops (FIG. 21-3F). Large washers on 1/4-inch bolts can secure the strap in a position that allows the feet to be slipped in and out.

Sliding Seat

The seat is shown as a flat board. In a racing boat the seat is shaped so the oarsman's buttocks fit without risk of slipping. It may be possible to get one of these seats or one intended for a kayak and screw it on. Many of these seats are made of fiberglass. Alternatively, use the flat board, but put half round molding across at front and back and use a thin mat to prevent slipping.

The top (FIG. 21-3G) may be solid wood or a piece of 3/4-inch plywood. Underneath, at each side, are a pair of wheels (FIG. 21-3H) guided on a track by angle iron supports.

The tracks are pieces of 1/4-inch-by-1-inch steel strip over the inner edges of the wood sides (FIG. 21-2A). Screw them at about 3-inch intervals, with the heads countersunk below the surface.

Turn the wheels wide enough to fit over the tracks and with bosses on each side (FIG. 21-3J). Drill for 3/8-inch axles.

The supports can be cut from 2-inch-by-3-inch-by-1/4-inch angle iron. All parts can be left 2 inches wide under the seat or the width reduced slightly (FIG. 21-3K). The inner guides extend downwards to overlap the track, but the outer angles are reduced to 2 inches (FIG. 21-3L).

Drill for axles 1 1/4 inch down. Position the guides under the seat board so the inner ones travel easily inside the tracks without wobble, and the outer ones give enough clearance for the wheels. Three screws with countersunk heads on top and nuts underneath will hold each angle. Bolts through will form axles for the wheels. Alternatively, the inner holes could be tapped and the outer holes drilled clearance size, so axles could be screwed in. Whichever method is used, make sure the wheels revolve on plain cylinders and not on screw threads.

Outriggers

The pivots or *fulcrums* for the oars or handles have to be supported 12 inches out from the framework sides and 6 inches above them. The outriggers that provide the supports (FIG. 21-2B) can be made from 1/4-inch-by-1-inch steel strip.

The outer assembly may be built up by bending one piece above another (FIG. 21-4A). Make the gap at least 1 inch. The pivot bolt (FIG. 21-4B) can be 1/4-inch diameter. The parts are joined with 1/4-inch bolts or rivets.

Set out the two views of the struts (FIG. 21-4C, D) to get the angles and lengths. The pivot has to be tilted outwards. It is shown at 15° to vertical (FIG. 21-4E), which should suit most users. Bend the tops of the struts to suit (FIG.

21-4F), and the other ends go downwards to take bolts through the sides (FIG. 21-4G). Slight variations from the given sizes will not matter, but make sure the opposite assemblies match and make a true pair to each other.

Oars

The two oars fit loosely on their pivots, so they can be moved up and down as the user pulls them: a motion similar to rowing a boat. This also allows for different heights of users.

Each oar is made up of a 1/4-inch steel strip bolted to wood, which simulates a normal oar, with a grip at the end. As the oars swing, they should come within about 2 inches of each other when square across (FIG. 21-2C),

The metal parts (FIG. 21-4H) have three positions for the spring cords, so loads can be varied. With the cords in the end holes, the oars are harder to pull than when the cords are further in. The pivot hole could be 5/16-inch and countersunk on both sides for easy movement on the bolt. The other holes are for 1/4-inch bolts into the wood parts.

Make the wood parts (FIG. 21-4J) of hardwood 1 3/4-inch square. Turn down the grips 5 inches long to 1 1/4-inch diameter and notch the underside to take the metal parts. Round the exposed edges.

Bolt the wood and metal parts together and try the action of the oars on the pivot bolts.

Spring Assembly

There is a bank of four springs arranged 2 inches apart below the seat. These should be the type used in physical training equipment. They are tension springs about 9 inches long, with loop ends. Four of the normal type should satisfy the strength of an athletic man. If less resistance is needed, the attachments to the oars can be moved in or one or more springs disconnected.

A piece of 1-inch-by-1-inch-by-1/8-inch angle iron 9 inches long will take the inner ends of the springs (FIGS. 21-2D, 21-5A). Three bolts through the central wood crosspiece should take

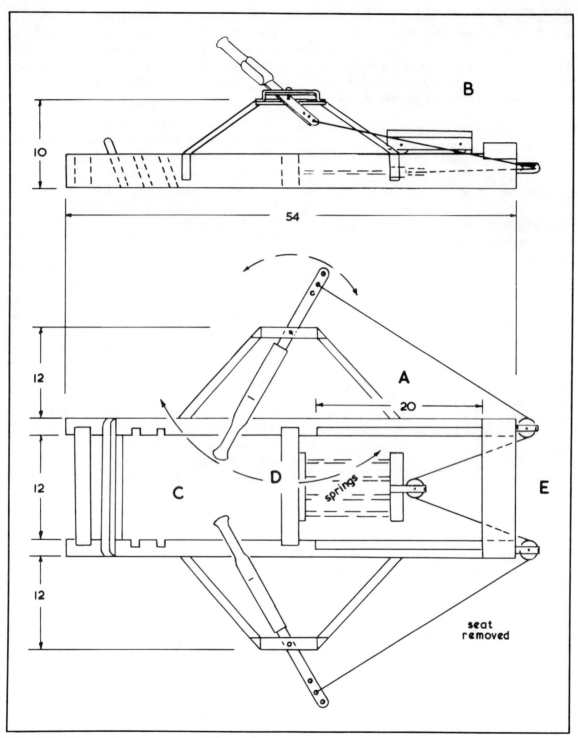

FIG. 21-2. Sizes and arrangements of the rowing exerciser.

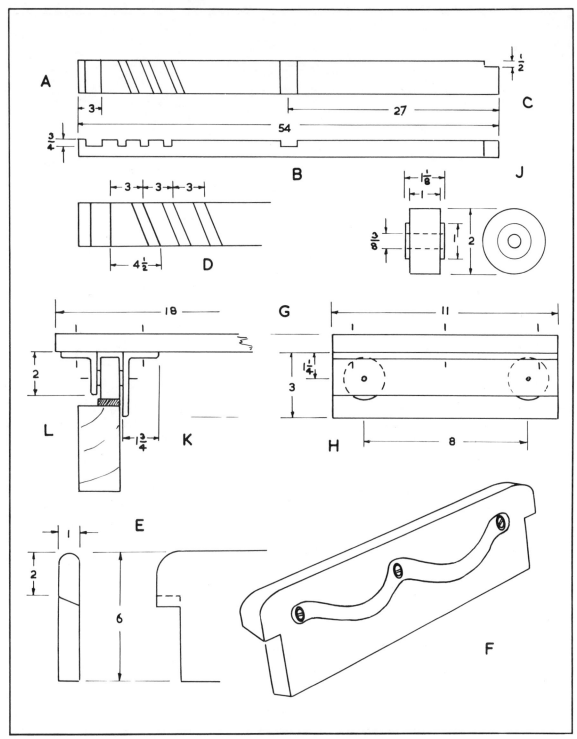

FIG. 21-3. The framework, seat, and footrest parts for the rowing exerciser.

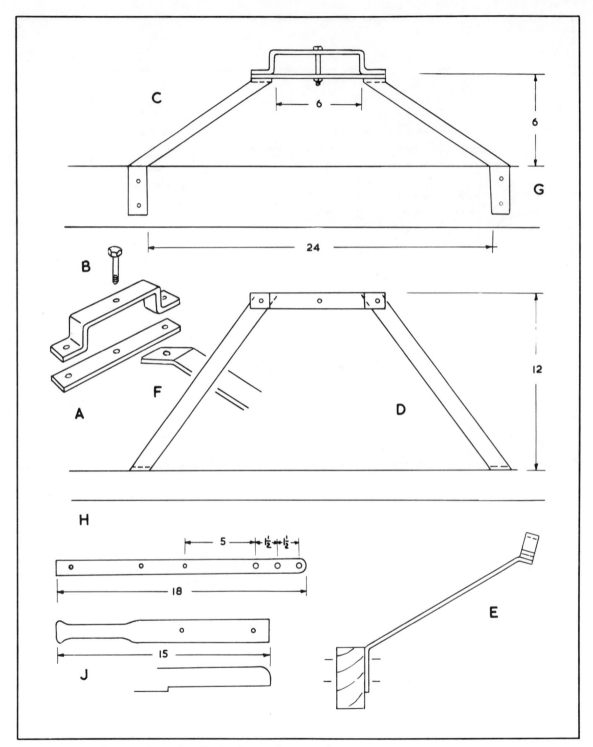

FIG. 21-4. Outrigger and oar details for the rowing exerciser.

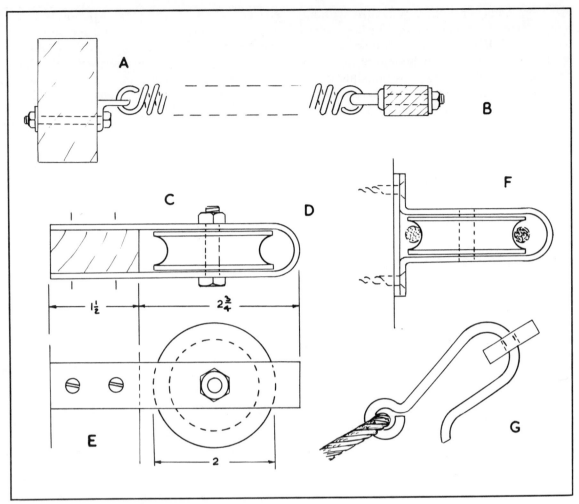

FIG. 21-5. Springs and pulleys for the rowing exerciser.

the strain. The other ends of the springs hook into eyebolts through a strip of 3/4-inch-by-1 1/2-inch wood (FIG. 21-5B).

Three pulleys have to be provided—one at the center of this bar and one on each of the ends of the sides (FIG. 21-2E). The central pulley is needed to allow for uneven pulls on the oars.

Make the pulleys with grooves deeper and wider than the rope that will pass through them (FIG. 21-5C, F), because the angle the rope makes will vary with different positions of the oars. For rope of 1/4-inch or 5/16-inch diameter, the grooves could be 1/2 inch wide. Make sure there is no roughness that could damage the rope.

At the center of the wood attached to the springs, make a loop to hold the pulley (FIG. 21-5D), leaving only enough space to pass the rope between the pulley and the wood to reduce the risk of the rope coming out of the groove. Strip steel 1/16-inch-by-3/4-inch will make the loop (FIG. 21-5E).

Other pulleys can be supported by loops made of similar strips at the ends of the sides (FIG. 21-5F). Make baseplates and turn out the ends of the loops so wood screws can be driven.

The ends of the rope may be knotted through the holes in the metal parts of the oars, but it would be better to make hooks (FIG. 21-5G).

Rope positions can then be changed without having to readjust rope length. The hooks may be made of 5/16-inch steel rod. One end of the rope may be spliced to its hook, but the other end should be knotted, to allow for adjustment.

When you have experimented with the exerciser and are satisfied that it performs as required, the wood may be stained and varnished and the metal parts painted, or all parts painted. The oar grips are best left as bare wood, which they would be on boat oars, to provide a better grip and reduce the risk of blisters!

22
Screw Jack

A means of lifting a short distance with considerable power is useful in many circumstances. There are many places where a heavy load has to be lifted or moved horizontally or at an angle. A thrust or lift can be applied, then the object supported in some way, while the power is applied over a packing for further movement. A screw jack can exert considerable power, but like many other means of applying mechanical advantage, you cannot expect both power and much movement.

This screw jack (FIG. 22-1) will lift or thrust from a closed position of about 12 inches to an open position of 16 inches. Its capacity will depend on the materials and quality of construction, but the design envisages a load of 1 ton.

All parts are mild steel. The lever would be better of tool steel, with the reduced end hardened and tempered.

The screw, which does the work, is 1 1/2-inch diameter. Its efficiency and the weight that can be lifted depends on the thread form. For the best results, it should be a square thread, either 3/16-inch or 1/4-inch. The narrower

thread should exert more power, but the wider one will not need as many turns for a given lift. The difference is slight and either will be satisfactory. If you do not have the equipment for cutting internal and external square threads, you could use Acme or buttress threads. If you have to use V threads, the jack will work satisfactorily, but it cannot exert as much power. Decide carefully on the thread to be used, because this will affect some details of construction.

The drawings show parts joined with screws. Some or all joints could be welded instead of screwed. Obviously, strong construction is essential. It is the top block of the tripod which takes the load. The lower triangular block steadies the legs and keeps the screw upright.

The tripod (FIG. 22-2A) is shown 10 inches high and with a spread of feet over 5 inches diameter. The angle and spread or size of feet could be increased, but this should be enough. It is usual to put a solid pad under the jack if the ground is uneven or soft.

Start with the screw (FIGS. 22-2B, 22-3A), which is turned from solid stock. The peg (FIG.

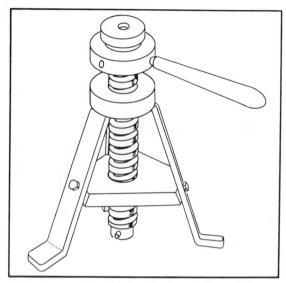

FIG. 22-1. A tripod screw jack.

Set out the shape of the legs (FIG. 22-2F), which are made from 3/8-inch-by-1 1/2-inch strip. Draw the angle (FIG. 22-2G) and mark the shapes of the ends. At the top of each leg (FIG. 22-2E), drill for 3/8-inch screws into the top block. Round the outer corners of the feet (FIG. 22-2H). Mark inside the legs where the triangular block is expected to come, but do not mark or drill any holes yet.

The triangular block (FIG. 22-3H) is drawn on a 2 1/4-inch radius circle, but check the actual size on a temporary assembly of the legs and top block. Differences in leg angles may not matter, providing this is allowed for when making the block. The three faces of the block that meet the legs should each be wider than a leg (FIG. 22-2K) and cut at an angle to suit. The edges between the legs may be left square or rounded. Cut a thread through the central hole to match the screw.

The pad (FIG. 22-3J) is turned with a taper towards the boss. The angle is not important, but is shown 30°. The hole fits over the peg above the boss and revolves on it, but is not attached to it.

When the jack is assembled and in use, the screw has to move smoothly through top and bottom blocks, so these threaded holes must be compatible. You cannot vary the top block, but you may have to move the triangular block up or down slightly to get the thread true. At the most, this would not be more than the pitch of a thread, and probably much less. Put matching marks on the block and a leg, so you reassemble in the same way.

Assemble the parts and ascertain the location of the triangular block on each leg when the screw can be rotated smoothly. Drill for 3/8-inch screws at each position (FIG. 22-2L) and assemble with the central screw holding the parts in position. Put the peg through the end of the screw when you are satisfied with the action.

The tripod may be painted, but the moving parts should be left bare and frequently lubricated in use.

22-3B) is to fit in the hole in the pad, which should revolve easily on it. Turn down the part to be threaded and reduce its end to the core size of the thread (FIG. 22-3C). This takes a 1/4-inch pin through (FIG. 22-3D), after assembly, to prevent the screw being lifted out of the lower block.

The holes in the boss (FIG. 22-3E) should be taken fairly deeply so there is little risk of the lever pulling out. The lever could be just a 1/2-inch rod, but it is better to turn down a piece of 3/4-inch rod (FIG. 22-2C), which will provide a more comfortable grip. Do not have an abrupt change of section, which would make a weak point. Reduce with a curve, as shown, and taper the end for easy entry into the holes, which may be lightly countersunk to remove sharp edges. Round the edges of the boss.

Cut the thread as close to the boss as your equipment will allow. You may wish to delay completion of the thread until you make the other parts, so threads can be matched.

The top block (FIG. 22-2D) is a turned circle (FIG. 22-3F), bored and threaded to match the central screw. The three legs are joined to it with screws (FIG. 22-2E) into equally spaced holes (FIG. 22-3G) or by welding.

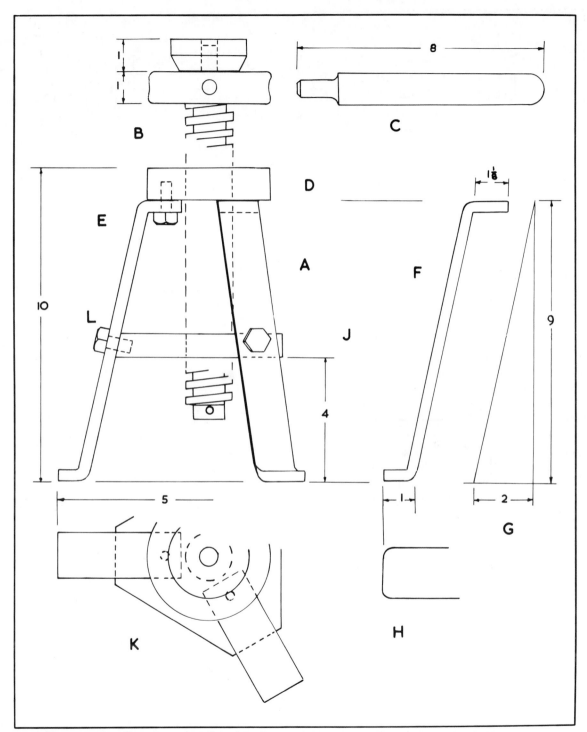

FIG. 22-2. Suggested sizes and layout of the screw jack.

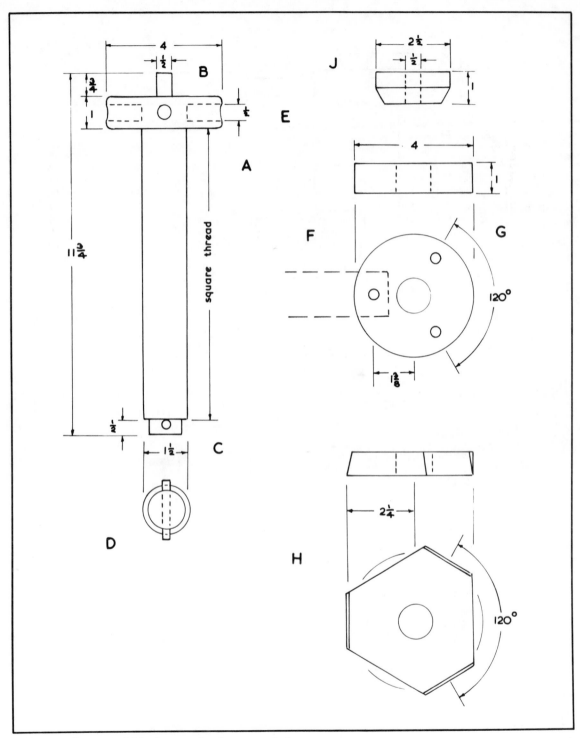

FIG. 22-3. Screw and block parts for the screw jack.

23

Folding Trolley

Most of us sometimes need to move loads which are too heavy to carry far, and some sort of light transport on wheels would be welcomed. The load may be a garbage can, a propane tank, a large water container, or a box of garden produce. The problem with many carts, trucks, and trolleys is the space they take up when you are not using them, so a folding trolley has some attraction.

This folding trolley (FIG. 23-1A) can be handled by one person, it will stand level, it will take a can or tank and be quite rigid in use, but when you want to pack it away, it will fold flat. The handle slides and folds on the back, which can be folded flat on the bottom. The thickness is less than 6 inches, and the length and width about 22 inches by 18 inches (FIG. 23-1B), respectively.

Most of the parts are 1-inch-by-1-inch-by-1/8-inch angle iron. The choice of wheels will depend on the intended use. They could be made, but those suggested are solid hard rubber, 6 inches in diameter and 2 inches thick, run-

ning on a 1/2-inch diameter axle. Wheels of this type will travel over soft ground with little risk of sinking in. Construction is shown with bolts or rivets. Some parts could be welded if you prefer that. For most joints, the rivets or bolts may be 1/4-inch diameter.

The general drawing shows that the base (FIG. 23-2A) has two sides joined with angle irons and carrying the axle and lugs that make the trolley stand level. On this is hinged a back (FIG. 23-2B), made of four uprights with strips across (FIG. 23-2C). The handle (FIG. 23-2D) fits between two of these uprights (FIG. 23-2E).

The key parts, which should be made first, are the pair of base sides (FIG. 23-2A), made of 1-inch-by-2-inch-by-1/8-inch angle iron, with the 2-inch legs upright. The end hole is for the axle. The next one to it is for the pivot, which could be 5/16-inch in diameter. The other holes are for attaching the crosspieces.

At the outer ends are the lugs (FIG. 23-3B). As shown, they suit 6-inch wheels, but you will have to modify the height for other wheels.

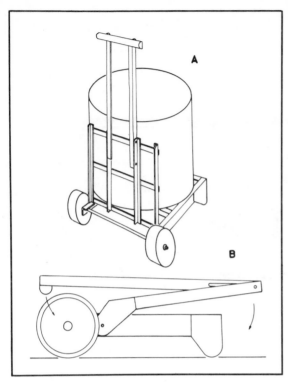

FIG. 23-1. A folding trolley will carry a large or heavy load (A), but can be packed flat (B).

holes are for bolts or rivets into matching holes on the uprights.

The four back uprights are the same length. They all have holes on the forward faces to take the strips across (FIG. 23-3G). The other legs of the pair of outer uprights only have holes for attaching to the pivot plates (FIG. 23-3H). Use countersunk rivets or bolts in the plate to give clearance for the wheels. The pair of inner uprights (FIG. 23-3J) have two holes linking to the handle. Delay drilling them until you make the handle sides.

The strips across (FIG. 23-2G) are pieces of 1/8-inch-by-1-inch section (FIG. 23-4A). Check their lengths and hole positions against other parts. Use bolts or rivets with countersunk heads at the front.

The suggested height of the handle is 36 inches above the floor, which should be convenient for controlling the loaded trolley, and it keeps the extension length within the folded size of other parts. Make a pair of handle sides (FIG. 23-3K). The slot has to slide on a 5/16-inch screw. Make set screws and washers to screw into the top holes of the uprights (FIG. 23-3J), with enough clearance for the handles to slide easily (FIG. 23-4B). These do not have to be removed for folding the handle, but the holes in the sides that match the other ends of the slot are for fastenings that have to be withdrawn, so the handle can be slid along for folding. You could use similar set screws with knurled heads (FIG. 23-4C). Another way would be to make pins with turn-over ends (FIG. 23-4D). A cord through a hole in each would allow them to be tied to the frame to prevent loss.

The top of the handles is shown with a crossbar (FIG. 23-2H). Comfort would be improved if a round wooden rod has a flat planed on it so it can be screwed on (FIG. 23-4E). An alternative handle would be a 1/2-inch steel rod welded across (FIG. 23-4F).

The axle is a 1/2-inch diameter rod long enough to extend through the wheels. There will have to be packings (FIG. 23-4G) to give clearance between the wheels and the pivot plates.

They take up one of the crosspiece holes and another drilled further along.

The three crosspieces are the same (FIG. 23-2F). They fit between the sides, so must have one flange cut away at each end (FIG. 23-3C), then the other bent to fit inside. The length (FIG. 23-3D) determines the sizes of some other parts. Join the sides and crosspieces.

The pivot plates (FIG. 23-3E) may be 1/8-inch plate. They link the outer uprights of the back with the sides of the base, so the back will fold down. As shown, there is ample clearance for 1/8-inch thick strips across the back. If you use strips of a different thickness, the horizontal measurements will have to be altered.

An optional piece is shown dotted (FIG. 23-3F). If this is included, the pair can be bent outwards to prevent the load swinging to the side and touching a wheel. The pivot bolt can be 1/4-inch or 5/16-inch diameter. The other two

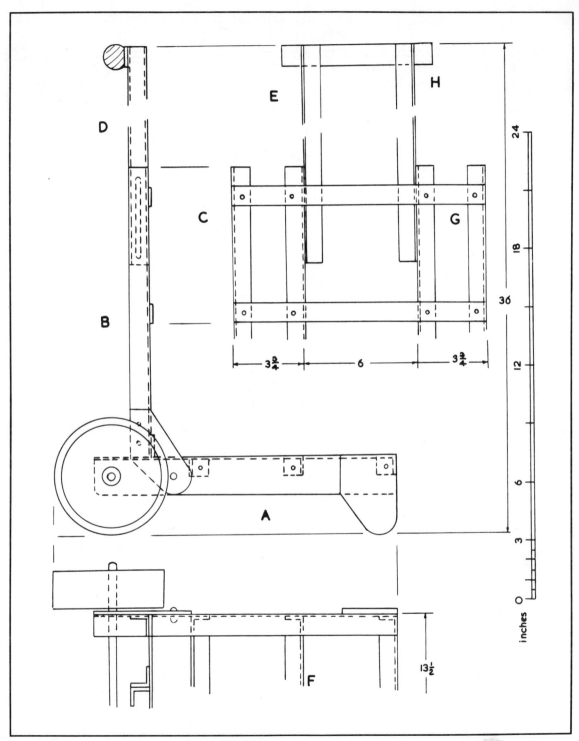

FIG. 23-2. Sizes and general arrangement of the folding trolley.

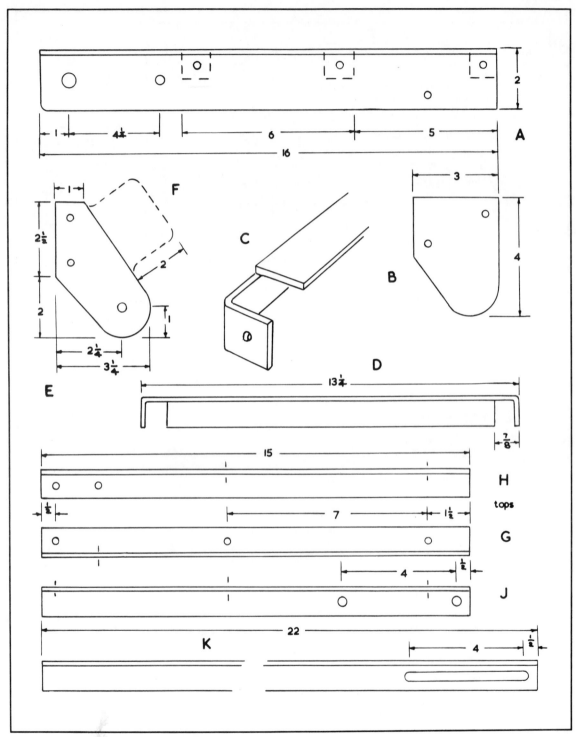

FIG. 23-3. Main parts of the framework of the folding trolley.

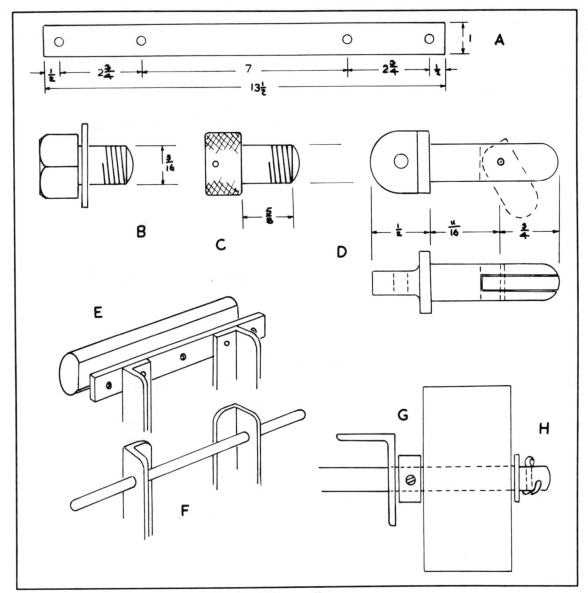

FIG. 23-4. Handle and turned parts for the folding trolley.

They may be loose or with screws locking them to the axle. How the wheels are attached may depend on their type, but for plain wheels, there can be washers and split pins through the axle (FIG. 23-4H).

Take sharpness and roughness off any exposed edges and corners. Try the folding action,

then partially dismantle and paint all over. A wood handle can be varnished or left plain. How your load is secured will depend on its type and shape, but straps or ropes can be attached at several places, without the need for special attachment points.

24
Extending Ladder Mechanism

A one-piece ladder of more than a moderate length becomes an unwieldly piece of equipment to handle and is often difficult to store. For use about the home, it is better to obtain the total length you need by arranging the ladder in two parts. This could be done with quite a small ladder to close short enough to stand in the garage. It might be a longer ladder that extends to a considerable height. A further advantage of having a ladder in two parts is that of being able to use them as separate short ladders. For the two sections to link safely at any extension, there have to be metal fittings that are secure, yet allow adjustment. This applies whether the ladder is wood or metal.

Some very long sectional ladders have to be operated with rope, but for use about the home it should be possible to get a sufficient height with two parts that can be extended by hand. For a person of average height to operate, the two parts can be up to 12 feet long; they then extend with a four-rung overlap to about 19 feet (FIG. 24-1A). With the extension handle suggested, it would be possible to have the two sections longer or for a shorter person to push the standard length without having to reach so far.

These instructions do not include the making of the ladders. It is assumed that these are wood, aluminum, or other metal. So that sizes can be given, it is assumed that the sides are 1-inch-by-3-inch section, and the rungs are 1-inch diameter and 10 inches apart, with the inner ladder 13 inches wide overall (FIG. 24-2A). The mechanisms are just as suitable for ladders of other sizes, but some dimensions will have to be altered.

A two-part short ladder needs a pair of retainers at the top of the outer part to keep the inner part in place (FIGS. 24-1B, 24-2B). At the lower end of the inner ladder, there are hooks to engage with rungs on the outer ladder (FIGS. 24-1C, 24-2C) at the position required. If you can reach to push up the ladder, that is all you need, but the extending handle (FIGS. 24-1D, 24-2D) can be added to increase the amount of movement.

The two parts of the ladder do not have to

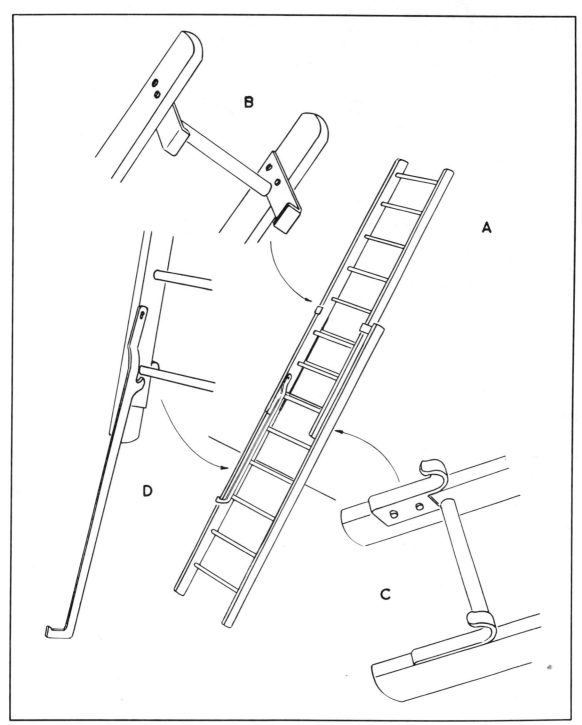

FIG. 24-1. The mechanism for an extending ladder (A) needs retainers (B) and hooks (C). There may be a handle (D).

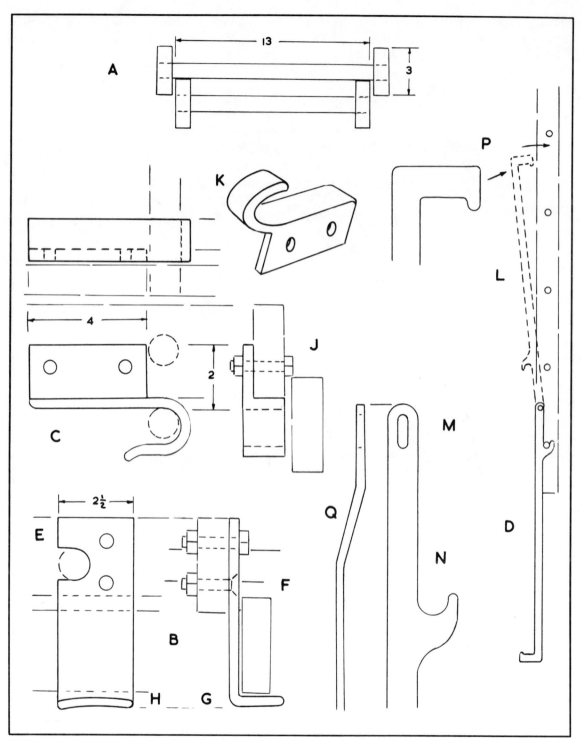

FIG. 24-2. Sizes and details of the metal parts for an extending ladder mechanism.

be made so one fits in the other closely. It is better if they can move freely, and at least 3/4-inch between the outside of the inner ladder and the inside of the outer one is usual. This allows fittings of adequate thickness to be used between the surfaces. For a very short ladder, the metal may be 1/4-inch thick. For ladders with greater extensions, it would be better at 5/16-inch or 3/8-inch. Parts should be attached with bolts through—usually the diameter may be the same as the thickness of the metal. If possible, use hexagonal heads, but where clearance is insufficient, they may be countersunk. When attaching to wood, do not drill any larger than is necessary to drive the bolts in, and use large washers under the nuts.

The pair of retainers should be located at the top rung of the outer section, and they may be notched over the rung (FIG. 24-2E), so it helps in taking the load. Make the length enough to allow the inner section side to slide with 1/2-inch clearance over the rung (FIG. 24-2F). Turn over the end so the overlap is enough to cover the inner section side (FIG. 24-2G), even when the ladder parts move in relation to each other. Curve the end (FIG. 24-2H) and well round the edges, particularly if the ladder is wood, for ease of extending and to reduce rubbing. The inner bolt head may have to be countersunk.

The pair of hooks on the inner part are bolted on below the bottom rung (FIGS. 24-1C, 24-2C). They come inside and overlap to the full width of the ladder side (FIG. 24-2J). It is possible to cut them from 2-inch-by-2-inch-by-5/16-inch or 3/8-inch angle iron, or they may be bent from sheet steel. Cut back angle iron so the hook can be made (FIG. 24-2K) to slip easily over a rung. Turn out the end of the hook and round its edges. Round other edges, particularly where they could catch on a rung when being moved into position.

The extension handle shown (FIG. 24-2D) is 33 inches long and projects about 20 inches below the inner part in use, but can be folded into the ladder when not required (FIG. 24-2L). It does not have to carry a load, other than the thrust up, so could probably be made from 1/4-inch steel. If the projections are welded on, it may be made from 1-inch strip. Otherwise, it must be cut from wider material. It is shown with a pivot midway between the last two rungs and the end folding below another rung. Check if this will suit your ladder.

At the pivot, there is a slot to fit over a 5/16-inch bolt (FIG. 24-2M). At the rung position, make a hook to fit around it (FIG. 24-2N). Make the slot long enough to allow the hook to move from fitting closely to disengaged.

The grip should not be bigger than the width of the ladder side (FIG. 24-2P) so that when the handle folds against the rungs, the grip does not project and touch the rungs of the other part. Well round it. If the end hook is inside the ladder side, crank the handle (FIG. 24-2Q) to pass over it.

Paint all the metal parts, including the bolt through holes, if they are not plated or galvanized.

Index

N1373